THE
UNEXPECTED
PATRIOT

THE
UNEXPECTED
PATRIOT

HOW AN ORDINARY AMERICAN MOTHER
IS BRINGING TERRORISTS TO JUSTICE

SHANNEN ROSSMILLER

WITH SUE CARSWELL

palgrave
macmillan

THE UNEXPECTED PATRIOT
Copyright © Shannen Rossmiller, 2011

First published in 2011 by PALGRAVE MACMILLAN® in the United States—a division of St. Martin's Press LLC, 175 Fifth Avenue, New York, NY 10010.

Where this book is distributed in the United Kingdom, Europe, and the rest of the world, this is by Palgrave Macmillan, a division of Macmillan Publishers Limited, registered in England, company number 785998, of Houndmills, Basingstoke, Hampshire RG21 6XS.

Palgrave Macmillan is the global academic imprint of the above companies and has companies and representatives throughout the world.

Palgrave® and Macmillan® are registered trademarks in the United States, the United Kingdom, Europe, and other countries.

ISBN: 978-0-230-10255-2

Library of Congress Cataloging-in-Publication Data
Rossmiller, Shannen.
    The unexpected patriot : how an ordinary American mother is bringing terrorists to justice / Shannen Rossmiller.
        p.   cm.
    Includes index.
    ISBN 978-0-230-10255-2 (hardback)
    1. Rossmiller, Shannen.   2. Undercover operations—United States.   3. Terrorism—United States—Prevention.   I. Title.
HV8080.U5R67   2011
363.325'163092—dc22
[B]
                                                                2011013307

A catalogue record of the book is available from the British Library.

Design by Letra Libre

First edition: September 2011

10 9 8 7 6 5 4 3 2 1

Printed in the United States of America.

To those who died on 9/11,
those who survived, and their families.

To our soldiers in the U.S. military who fight for
freedom and against terrorism at home and abroad.

To the FBI generally and specifically to Special Agent
Mark Seyler. S.A. Seyler embodies the FBI's motto
of "Fidelity, Bravery, Integrity" and has been my
guardian angel as I have navigated the path in helping
to pioneer the field of cyber-counterintelligence.

It is in your memory and honor that I fight this fight and
will continue until the threat of terrorism is defeated.

CONTENTS

INTRODUCTION

The glass doors in front of me are the only thing keeping the rabid media from pouncing. Suddenly, I realize that once I leave the building, my life will never be the same again and I can't control a rush of emotion. It's not like me to show my feelings publicly, yet I'm crying uncontrollably. I am terrified of what lies ahead.

Only a few hours ago, my life seemed manageable, even under the stress and strife of this case. Now, I don't know what to do. I know there is only one way out of the building that would allow me to run from this madness and find a safe place to hide—like the forts and shelters I stole away to as a child on my parents' farm in Montana, in retreat from the real world. Yet I cannot bring myself to cross the threshold before me. I am already grieving for my former life.

Since that infamous day in September 2001, where nearly three thousand lives were lost at the hands of al-Qaeda terrorists, my life has taken a direction I did not consciously choose or anticipate. But my parents taught me that when you are called upon to do a duty, you step up to the challenge and make the best of what life hands you. This maxim is why I find myself here at Fort Lewis today. However, it's easier said than done.

CHAPTER ONE

WHEN FIRST WE MET

I am spinning around, staring up at the bluish gray sky, as I would back home in rural Montana. I am in New York City for the first time and my senior class is now on the 110th floor of the south tower, on the World Trade Center's observation deck. I look down, clutching the steel fence and marveling at the 1,377 feet below, between me and the ground. In Conrad, Montana, the tallest objects are silos and grain elevators. Just as in Big Sky Country, I can see for miles, all the way to the New Jersey skyline. The people look like little ants. I clutch a pin of the towers that I purchased to commemorate this special day atop the tallest buildings in the world. When I peek over the edge, I hear our trip's narrator say, "If you drop a penny from this height and it hits someone on the head, it could penetrate them, hurting or maybe even killing them." I hold on to the pennies in my spring coat tightly. I am not here to cause harm. It feels like the building is leaning, which doesn't scare me; it's strange but exciting. Because it's March, my allergies are acting up terribly. It is humid and raining slightly. My eyes are burning.

On 9/11, when I got home from work, I went into my keepsake box and found the pin I had bought that day. I taped it to my computer. It was a concrete reminder of what had happened. Watching the towers fall over and over again on TV affected my whole being. It still does. I think daily of the wanton destruction, the fire, the dust, the twisted steel—the sheer carnage caused by a group of terrorists led by bin Laden who felt justified in the name of Allah to do harm to thousands of innocent people.

I have my other identities, too. I am Abu Abdullah, an al-Qaeda courier. My name is Abu Latif, and I am a recruiter trainer. I am Abu Musa. I have weapons and supplies. My name is Abu al Haqq, and I am an al-Qaeda financier. My name is Abu Zeida. I am located in Af-Pak. I am radicalized, a bloodthirsty mujahideen . . .

But I'm jumping ahead of myself. Let's start from the beginning.

So much of who we are comes from how we were raised. For me, it was on a farm and ranch in Montana.

I was born a fighter, a "little scrapper" of sorts. I came into this world early, as a premature baby. I had a rare Rh-blood disorder, which meant I wasn't producing any white blood cells, and the nuns had to draw blood every day until my body started making them. This took a month. As a result, I never learned to sleep, a problem that haunts me to this day.

When my parents brought me home, I was so small that my dad placed me in a shoebox to show their friends and family. I was fed with a doll's bottle and had to wear doll-sized clothes, since preemie clothes were not available then. The doctors told my parents that premature babies tend to be slower and have developmental issues. So they prepared themselves for that.

I lived-up to the nickname, Little Scrapper, becoming strong and determined. I sat up, spoke, and walked ahead of schedule. I could run before I was a year old. I was so small, I didn't have to duck to get under the kitchen table, and I raced to follow my dad, whom I adored, wherever he went. I was always restless, fearless, and in search of adventure. The comfortable world my parents provided allowed me to flex my endless imagination, which imbued every day with endless possibility. At age three, when my father told me I couldn't go to town with him, I hid in the back of his pickup truck, surfacing halfway down the highway when my fingers went numb with the cold and my cheeks hovered dangerously close to frostbite.

I learned how to read at a very young age. This wasn't a huge surprise, once the preemie fears were allayed: my parents are intelligent people. My mom, Reba, was a teacher, and my dad, Darrell, was a rancher and wheat farmer who enlisted in the Navy after high school. My father was so handsome that he could have played the hero in a Western movie. At harvest time, I marveled at how he marshaled the men and the machines like a general on a battlefield.

No place could have been freer or more exciting for a kid than the twenty-eight hundred acres my family owned in the plains east of Conrad. Outside the big brick farmhouse, I found what seemed like endless barns, bunkhouses, haystacks, and fields to explore. In fact, my parents would lock me in my room at night to prevent me from wandering too far. Undaunted, I began climbing out my bedroom window to continue my nightly adventures.

I was determined to sleep anywhere but my bed. I'd sleep in my closet, a bathtub, or out in the garden in the flowerbeds. My parents would say, "Where are we going to find her now?" In fact, one night when my parents could not find me in any of my usual places they became very concerned and called around to neighbors to help search. They eventually found me asleep in the sleeper cab of my dad's Peterbilt semi truck.

I had forts all around the farm, which I built near the shelterbelts that were planted at intervals to break the prairie wind and keep the soil from blowing away. I had a Flintstones fort where I drew images of the characters—I especially liked Bam-Bam and Dino—and taped them on the large rock that served as the door to the fort. I had a Brady Bunch fort, one for the Swiss Family Robinson, and one very close to my heart based on the television show *Emergency One,* starring the paramedics John and Roy. I even made forts in the haystacks, until my mother told me that sometimes rattlesnakes liked to sleep there.

One of my mom's favorite stories is about a time when we were coming home from Conrad to the farm after shopping one day. I was upset that she didn't get one of the things that I wanted for dinner that night. I was particularly peeved because I had invited John and Roy to come to dinner. I was standing up in the front seat of our Suburban, adamant that we had to treat our guests well. She wasn't taking me seriously, so I told her that when we got home, I was going to run away. (I was three and a half.) After we got home, I packed up my belongings and headed out the front door, only to sit down at the end of the driveway. My mom watched me for a long time through the kitchen window. And when she finally came out and said, "I thought you were going to run away!" I said, "How can I run away when I'm not allowed to cross the road yet?" That was the extent of my protest.

I found relief in my forts. I felt at peace. One day, my dad brought home a red Honda 70 three-wheeler, which allowed me to get to my forts, some of which were as far as a mile and a half away from the farm (this was in the days before ATVs). I had a matching red helmet with gold sparkles on top. I remember the incredible sense of freedom and excitement that day brought.

My forts were private, and I was fiercely protective of them—I did not want to share them with other kids. When I was three and a half, my parents put me in a Montessori preschool in Great Falls that I attended three days a week. This was not long after my brother, Aaron, was born. I wasn't hyperactive, but I think my mother needed time to attend to my newborn brother, who was born with the same Rh-blood disorder I was born with, and it was probably also a way to rein me in. In Montessori school, I would learn French and more formal reading skills, as well as tap and ballet. My mother was a tap and ballet dancer her whole life, so she approved of this effort to socialize me with feminine activities. The one thing my parents did not anticipate from the Montessori school experience was having this little French-speaking thing with no one to talk to back home. They couldn't understand a word.

My mom says I was born five years old. When I was a kid, I would rather hang around and talk with adults than with other children. One of my clearest memories growing up was the Sunday night ritual of watching *60 Minutes*. As soon as I heard the "tick, tick, tick" of the broadcast's intro, I was right there on my dad's lap. I was also fascinated by the nightly evening news and the larger world outside our farm. When the American hostages were taken in Iran in 1979, and the news media counted the days, I remember thinking, "That is so many days—when is this going to stop?" I can still recall the TV images of the era, as well as the last days of the Vietnam War and the airlifts. I even remember the Watergate scandal.

Ever since, I've had a keen interest in current affairs, news, history, and culture. One of my other favorite things growing up was the *Childcraft Encyclopedia* set my parents gave me. It introduced me to fascinating subjects including the Civil War, ancient Egypt, the ancient Greeks and Romans, and so on.

My other favorite pastime as a youngster took place on Saturdays in the spring and summer—cow slaughtering. I loved to sit on the fence post, and I couldn't wait for the sound of the rifle shooting the cow. Although I harbored this macabre fascination for the slaughtering ritual, I never stayed around to watch the butchering process, which entailed pulling the guts and innards from the dead cow.

My dad always had a book in hand, a habit he retains to this day. He likes true crime. My mom, on the other hand, was very stereotypically "feminine." She was in charge of the local Junior Miss pageant, and for seventeen years she did all of its choreography. Though I loved and admired my mother, it was my father whom I related to and found interesting. He would leave books in the grain trucks, combines, or his pickup, and when he went off marshaling his harvest crew I would grab them and wander through the pages and pictures. Once my dad finished a book, he would place it in the storage collection of boxes and paper grocery bags we had underneath the staircases in our home. Left alone and overcome with curiosity, I would sneak in and grab certain books to read secretly at night. In what marked the beginning of a lifelong pattern of compartmentalizing those interests that marked me as different, I protected my growing interest in the contents of my dad's books, because I knew they weren't meant for my impressionable eyes—especially with titles like *In Cold Blood* and *Helter Skelter*. I knew there was a reason they were underneath the stairs and not on the living room bookshelf. But I couldn't help myself.

One of the kinds of books I couldn't get enough of were those about serial killers. The first serial killer who caught my attention remains my favorite. Ted Bundy was a handsome guy. He was very charismatic and highly intelligent. I was eight when I first became aware of and interested in Bundy. To look at him you'd never know he was a killer, let alone a serial killer. In later years, when I read new books about Bundy, I learned that while traveling from Washington to Colorado, it was thought he had actually passed through Montana, and it was strangely exciting for me that he had once been so close.

What fascinates me about people like Bundy is their behavioral and psychological makeup. They know enough to hide what they're doing and they're aware that it's wrong, yet they have no conscience, so they do it again and again.

At the end of my fifth grade year, we had to do a project on things that were of interest to us. Most of my classmates presented on subjects such as the solar system, cooking, quilting, and so on. As I recall, their projects were age-appropriate but did not hold my interest. I was convinced that I had the best presentation, thinking, "Wow, have I got something!" I asked my teacher if I could make my presentation last. I truly believed that mine was going to knock them all out. I knew it was something that they wouldn't know anything about. I got up in front of my class with my three poster boards of Ted Bundy, Ed Gein, and John Wayne Gacy, who had all the little boys buried under his house. I started with Ted Bundy because he was handsome and happened to be on trial at the time down in Florida. I'd see reports of the trial on the news and thought he was a rock star. I next presented John Wayne Gacy, explaining how he dressed up as a clown to entertain at parties, and his interest in little boys. Finally, I told them how Ed Gein was the prototype for the movie *Psycho*. I described how Gein would skin women and place their remains over his dead mother.

I remember trying to point out how these individuals shared similar backgrounds and traits. Each suffered from childhood abuse, neglect, and isolation. Each felt that his obviously superior intelligence and appeal were not properly rewarded by society. Real and imagined insults and slights became justification for murder, ritualized and perverse. Not one of them possessed the kind of spiritual foundation that would have given him the strength or inspiration to reject the evil that boiled inside and to find a better path.

As I wrapped up, I was aware that I was not getting the response that I had expected. Everyone had clapped at the end of the other presentations, but not mine. I remember thinking, "Why are they looking at me like that?" The next day, I found out that the principal had received calls from concerned parents, and my mom and I had to meet with him in his office over the incident. He made sure I knew how inappropriate my presentation was. My mom had no idea of the subject matter of my presentation as I was left to do my schoolwork and projects mostly on my own. What I remember most was the one word consistently used to describe what I had done: "disturbing." I remember how surprised I was to be in trouble. I wasn't a trouble-making child.

My saving grace in the aftermath of this incident was that it was the end of the school year. That summer I hid away from the normal summer activities I loved, like swimming at our local pool.

The experience of my class presentation reinforced the feeling that I was different, even a little strange. It taught me to be careful about sharing my true self. I came to believe that if you want to get along, it's not a good idea to show too much intensity or individuality. It makes people uncomfortable, and they may reject you. I went through the rest of my public school years with my guard up. I tried to conform, and although I was ultimately accepted by my peers, it was lonely growing up because nobody ever knew me very well. I was too afraid of being judged or ostracized to let people get close to me. I still struggle with this today.

I always dreamed of going to law school and becoming a crusader, someone who could make a difference. Even though I withdrew my acceptance to law school to get married, I always felt that the profession was something that I would eventually pursue. In some ways, I think that dream fueled my desire to pursue Internet intelligence work, because it seemed so vitally important. It became my new dream to someday work my way so deep into the world of terrorism and counterintelligence that I could take out some high-value target terrorists.

The core of what motivates me is doing the right thing or righting wrongs when possible. I seek to gain and retain the respect of people I admire because that is important to me. If someone tells me I can't do something, I will instinctively seek to prove them wrong. I have no patience for negative people. I have a need to understand the world, and I will pursue something until I can understand it.

CONRAD IS A QUIET, PICTURE-POSTCARD kind of town, where families, churches, and schools are the nerve centers. Many locals have roots a century or more deep. I can count more than a hundred relatives in the area. The hardware stores, gas stations, and farm supply shops that line the two-lane highway leading into town are family-owned. The people you pass on the road wave hello. It is not uncommon for people there to fly flags on their front porches every day of the year.

I've known my former husband, Randy Rossmiller, since we were kids. His father, also a farmer, was friends with my dad, and our families got together from time to time. When I returned to Conrad from college, we moved in the same social circles. Randy was easy to talk to and very smart. But the first thing any woman would notice was that he was handsome in a very warm and approachable way. Tall and slender, he had soft brown teddy bear eyes, thick brown hair, and a friendly smile—he was a dead ringer for Ben Affleck in *Pearl Harbor.* We started dating in late 1992. In 1995, we married and moved into one of the houses on his family's farm. We have three children, a boy and two girls. We were a big busy family, part of a larger Rossmiller clan that was very close-knit—sometimes too close-knit.

Randy's father, Lawrence, passed away suddenly in March of 1989, leaving Randy and his two brothers to share the work and responsibility for the farm, which included supporting his aging mother. As with any family business, the operation came with plenty of stress and conflict, which sometimes spilled into our relationship. I loved Randy and I wanted our marriage to work, but the conflicts and strain within his family were too much for me to take. By 1999, the stress and pressure of the dynamic of being part of a family farming business had taken its toll. Because we lived 35 miles from the nearby town where our kids attended school, Dutton, they had an hour commute to and from school each day. In 1997, I returned to work in the legal field, taking a part-time position clerking for a local court, which led me to a full-time position with a law firm in Conrad in early 1998. By the time conflict started to brew with my family's farming business in late 1999, I had been working in Conrad for almost three years, which made it difficult to accommodate the kids' afterschool activities and interests as they went to school in Dutton. Over the summer of 1999, it was becoming more apparent that it was time for a change not only for the kids but for our family. Though it was a hard decision to make, I decided to move with the kids into Conrad to enroll them in school, which would also accommodate my job there. W decided to move into my deceased grandmother's home until we were able to find more formal living arrangements.

The move to Conrad was exciting for the kids and simplified life for me as a working mother, but it was also challenging as the move left Randy living at the farm and joining us a couple nights a week in Conrad while he wrapped up his exit from the family farming business. In early 2000, we decided to purchase a home in Conrad owned by my family. By March of that year, we were all united again.

I was sure the move would help us make it as a family. And at first, it did. Randy opened a business selling custom-made computer systems and wireless networking, which would grow slowly but steadily.

Randy was a self-taught technician, one of those gifted hands-on geniuses with almost anything mechanical. Back in 1995, when we got our first computer, Randy had basically no knowledge of or experience with computer systems or the complex components of networking. I like to tell a funny story that puts things into perspective regarding Randy's knowledge of computers back then to where it is today. Our first computer was purchased from his oldest brother, Dan, and his wife, Debbie. I had told Randy that if I was going to be staying at home after the birth of our youngest daughter, I would need a computer so I could do freelance legal work from home. We brought the 386 PC home, which came with the desktop unit and a monitor. The purchase was fine with me as it provided me with the Microsoft Office programs that I would need for my freelance work, but other than having a very antiquated Chuck Yeager flight simulator program there was really nothing there of interest to Randy. Then, one of the last days I was at work before I would be taking maternity leave, he called my office and asked how to turn the "damn thing on." Apparently Randy had decided that he wanted to see how the computer operated. I told him that the "on" button was located on the back of the desktop unit. Needless to say, but not to my surprise, when I got home from work that day, he had taken apart the entire guts of the desktop and had identified each part inside. I was not very happy at this scenario as I was not convinced that he hadn't just ruined the computer! But, he managed to put everything back together without incident within a couple of days, and the machine ran as if it had never been disturbed. From that day forward, Randy began the process of learning and mastering computer systems. In fact, he was the only computer tech who ever serviced or repaired that very first machine and each and every system he custom built and maintained. He has since been formally certified in many areas of the technology field. Soon he was building and repairing computers and network systems as well as wireless Internet networks.

In August of 1999, I was appointed as judge by the Conrad city council, as well as by the town of Valier. (Montana allows nonlawyers to serve on the bench if they have some legal background and are approved by the Montana Supreme Court.) In my time on the bench, I proudly served both jurisdictions.

Because of my ability to research and analyze, I took to my judgeship with passion and ease. Just as Randy was a natural when it came to understanding the mechanics of things, I naturally understood the law. Understanding its principles and maxims has always been something of a challenge, but I have relished this challenge and took on all its complexities happily. I truly loved being a judge and looked upon the responsibilities and authority that came with the job with respect and common sense. I never wanted to become one of those individuals who succumbed to what I call "black robe syndrome"—when individuals fail to separate themselves from the job and instead become the job. Because I was appointed to the bench at such a young age, I wanted the people of the communities I served to respect me as a judge and not see my young age as any sort of disadvantage.

At the time I was appointed to the bench, at twenty-nine, I was not aware that I was the youngest female municipal judge to be appointed in the history of the country. In fact, I didn't know this fact until I was profiled by the National Judicial College in 2005 for my cyber-intelligence work. My legal education and experience, along with passing a five-hour test, secured my appointment to the bench. As a judge I oversaw some civil cases, but my docket consisted primarily of criminal cases such as drug and alcohol offenses—especially the methamphetamine that had hit my community hard—petty thefts, assaults, traffic offenses, and animal control.

Ever since I first went into the law, I discovered a love for litigation, research, and writing—and making the winning argument. Though I was happy being a judge, I was also happy that it was not a full-time commitment and only required me to sit in court three days a week. It left me free to spend the rest of the workweek doing civil litigation work in the private sector working for my best friend, Chris Christensen, a private attorney and local prosecutor whom I had worked with since 1998.

SOME OF OUR BEST FAMILY TIMES came on weekend nights when I'd make my secret spaghetti recipe or scalloped potatoes and ham, and we'd all eat together and talk. After the dishes were done, Randy and I would go out to the garage, which we had turned into a kind of recreational room, and hang out like we were kids again. We'd listen to music from the '70s and '80s and play darts. On a Saturday or Sunday, Randy might work on one of his model airplanes—the kind that actually fly by remote control—or take one to a local field where he and his friends would fly them. He enjoyed this hobby so much, and back then it felt good just to watch him in action.

Sometimes the cases on my docket verged on the comical. That's what happened when the local animal control officer found an illegal python slithering loose in a house full of twenty-three illegal rats. The snake and the rats were required by law to receive due process, so we posted a five-day notice prior to their extermination. At the last minute, their owner appeared, disrupting the court by shouting, "Stop her! She's going to kill our babies!" I tried to solve the issue with reasoning and compassion but received nothing in return but angry shouts. Finally I slammed my gavel down and shouted, "The rats die today!"

I'd like to think I was a fair judge. I had a good reputation, and I was very careful not to overplay it. I considered the circumstances of the individual because each crime is, after all, only one moment in a person's life. Some judges are caught up in the thrill of having power, but I just wanted to be respected. Underneath my robe, I wore jeans or shorts. (I dread putting on a suit and—God forbid—high heels.) One of my most uncomfortable times on the bench was when my dad received a speeding ticket. He had called me at home after receiving the ticket, and he wanted it taken care of. I was kind of appalled that he would even think of asking me to do that. So when he called I simply said, "No. I can't treat you differently than I treat anybody else. Because the first time I do that, I'm dead in the water." I told him our conversation was bordering on improper because he had been cited with an offense and he was going to have to plead guilty or not.

I said, "I can't talk to you until the day you come to court."

I always processed speeding tickets starting at ten o'clock—first come, first served—but I purposely left my dad to the end. I had to read him his rights, which was awkward.

He said, "So you're really going to make me go through with this."

I said, "Dad, your choices are guilty or not guilty. Those are your options, and that's it."

Most unhappily, he paid the eighty-five-dollar fine and left my court.

CHAPTER TWO

HOUR BY HOUR

For as long as I can remember, I have always been a news junkie. After the 1993 World Trade Center bombing, I was watching some old footage of ABC's John Miller interviewing Osama bin Laden. I remember thinking, "Who the heck is this guy calling for a war on us?" I couldn't understand at the time why anyone would want that.

Going back to my years as a child on my parents' farm, it has always been my habit to rise early in the morning . . . usually around 4:00 a.m. On the morning of 9/11, I was up as usual at 4:00 a.m., researching and writing legal briefs in anticipation of things that might come before the court. Also, the TV is always on. I can't be in a quiet house; I even sleep with the TV on.

That morning I took my shower at six. I was sitting in our blue crushed velvet recliner, brushing my hair out. I knew I'd have to get the kids up soon. Suddenly, Katie Couric, anchor if the *Today* show, broke into the local news fifteen minutes early, saying they were getting word that a plane had hit one of the towers of the World Trade Center. Like a lot of people, I thought, "How the hell does that happen? It's the largest building in Manhattan." But as soon as the second one hit, I thought of bin Laden. I was transfixed, stricken with fear, anger, and confusion. I immediately began praying that God would help everyone directly affected, and our country, through this crisis.

I remember that day, hour for hour. As the kids got ready, I kept watching. Randy and I had been married long enough for him to know that I would have trouble pulling myself away from the television. I didn't have any hearings that day, just administrative things to do. I called my clerk, Gail, and said, "Please find a TV, or I'm staying home." I wasn't about to leave what was unfolding before my eyes. Gail went to the police department and borrowed a TV, and all day long we sat and watched, using rabbit ears to get reception. In hindsight, it's strange to me that people came to court as if it was a normal day.

Montanans tend to pay more attention to what is going on locally. I kept saying, "Wasn't that something?" and people would say, "Oh it's no big deal. I got sick of watching it." But to me it was profound, despite the fact that my only connection to the WTC was visiting years earlier with my class.

Randy was at the farm, and I had been trying to reach him all day. It pissed me off that night when he too said, "It's not that big of a deal." He was so flip about it. "You've had the whole day to be upset. It's time to get over it. Go take a Jacuzzi. Calm down."

I said, "But they are saying they may need as many as fifty thousand body bags for the people lost in the towers!"

I was now switching between CNN and MSNBC and rewatching Ashleigh Banfield and other reporters running from the smoke and the debris from the fallen towers. I kept saying, "Randy, this is huge." My son was sitting there with me, glued to it. The girls were too young to be aware of what was going on. But Randy was very nonchalant.

In that moment, one of the things that always separated us—how we react to serious events and challenges—was crystal clear. Randy tended to focus on what was close at hand, ignoring anything that didn't affect him directly. I, on the other hand, felt a powerful need to understand whatever was going on in the world and to take action, on my own, to make things better.

I finally decided to take a bath downstairs in our new Jacuzzi. I loved to read books in the bath. At the time, I was reading the Left Behind series based on the Book of Revelation. I was hooked. There were nine books in the series. I could get lost in them for hours at a time. So I filled up the tub, let it get really hot, and started the Jacuzzi. We had just put down ceramic tiling on the stairs leading up to the Jacuzzi, but there were no grip strips laid down on the tiling yet.

After an hour or so, I stepped out of the tub, wet and wobbly, and I slipped. I found myself on the floor and in immediate, excruciating pain. As the seconds became minutes, the pain got worse and worse. I tried to move enough to grab a towel off the towel rack, fearing one of the kids would open the door and find me naked on the floor. Our home office was directly above the downstairs bathroom, so I screamed for Randy over and over until he finally came charging down the stairs. He wrapped me up and carried me upstairs.

Every movement hurt. Randy laid me down on the couch and said, "Nothing's broken. Let's see how you are in the morning." So I thought maybe if I relaxed it would go away. But the pain just kept intensifying—and was worse any time I tried to move. I told him I thought I needed to go to the hospital and he said, "No. No." He was adamant.

Randy has never had anything medically traumatic happen to him. He assumed I'd just pulled a muscle or hurt my sciatic nerve and said, "Quit making a big deal out of it." All night I lay awake, furious with him. I sweated so much from the pain that my hair drenched the living room sofa, where I lay watching the unbelievable events continuing to unfold at Ground Zero.

I knew that my pain and discomfort didn't compare to what those devastated people were dealing with back east.

The next morning I screamed for Randy to get the kids up. I hadn't eaten, had anything to drink, or even used the bathroom. I told him I needed to go to the hospital. He said, "Shannen, it's going to be about five thousand dollars to go to the emergency room." Randy never had any real idea of what the cost might be but threw out large numbers to justify his refusal. We didn't have health insurance. Also, he had set up an appointment to have DSL Internet installed that day and was not going to miss that. The longer I lay there, the more angry I got. With my teeth gritted, I said, "I'm serious, Randy, this pain is only worse and not getting better—something is not right. I can't even will my legs to move." I was so damn mad at him. This was something that was not going to take care of itself.

After Randy had the kids off to school, he begrudgingly drove his pickup from around the back garage to the front of the house to get me to the emergency room and some desperately needed medical attention. Though the hospital was just a few blocks away, every bump in the street brought gasping pain. I gritted my teeth and held onto the armrest.

After having X-rays and a couple of hours of examination by doctors, I was told that I had suffered a hairline fracture to my pelvis—which could not be set and wrapped in a cast like a broken arm or leg. I was going to have to tough it out the old-fashioned way, waiting for the fracture to fuse itself. The doctor prescribed pain pills, muscle relaxers, and physical therapy over the next several weeks. I couldn't imagine lying in bed for so long. It sounded like a prison sentence. I didn't know how I was going to do it without going insane.

I would be away from work for several weeks, but I had the administrative work from the court as my workload at the private office, which Chris sent home for me to help pass the time recovering. And in these early days following 9/11, I found myself caught up in the constant news coverage. I became more and more affected by the tragedy and was getting angrier as the days wore on. It completely consumed me. I was changing inside.

Most people in Montana who live in smaller communities usually try to do their grocery and general needs shopping in one of the bigger cities because of the price disparity between local merchants and those in the cities. You'll pay seven bucks for twenty slices of cheese in Conrad—but if you did your shopping in the city, you could get seventy-two slices of cheese for around six dollars. So it was our routine to make the trek to Great Falls for weekly shopping.

While I was recovering, Randy made the trips alone, and every week I would prepare and give him a list of books I wanted him to pick up at Barnes & Noble. Whenever a talking head, scholar, or expert mentioned a book on TV that had something to do with al-Qaeda, bin Laden, the Taliban, or Islam, I asked Randy to pick me up a copy. I even had him order me an English translation of the Koran.

Over five weeks I read more than fifty books. I had a highlighter and sticky notes to mark interesting points I wanted to learn more about. My challenge to myself was to figure out where these people were coming from, to understand their teachings, their culture, and how their world differed from the West. All of these new things I was learning, coupled with the ongoing drama at Ground Zero and the global chaos following the 9/11 attacks, really drew me in—I was fascinated. When I have something in front of me, I can't half-ass it, I've got to kill it. I'll dog it until there's nothing left.

I was so consumed by my readings, and so angry and discouraged by my helplessness, that I began looking for a way to do something about it. I called the Air Force National Guard to see if I could volunteer after the United States and the coalition countries invaded Afghanistan in Operation Enduring Freedom on October 7.

With only the best intentions, I set up a time for a recruiter to come to the house and talk to me and Randy. I had received some brochures from the Air Force recruiter detailing what they had to offer and what could be expected. I had decided that I was interested in going into language training at the Defense Language Institute in Monterey, California. I could apply after basic training. To me, this path seemed both honorable and reasonable. That night, however, as we sat at the kitchen table, the recruiter discussed expectations and assignments I might be given, and laid out various items of paperwork. I asked a few questions, then advised the recruiter that I would discuss everything with Randy and would get back to him soon.

However, I should have seen what was coming. When the recruiter left, Randy had a fit. I'd hoped he would be happy and proud, but as with the failed serial-killer school presentation back in fifth grade, I had completely miscalculated the outcome of my actions. He was furious. "You're not going to the National Guard, Shannen!" he screamed. "You have three kids and a husband, for Christ's sake! You're not in a position to take on something like this. This has gone far enough, Shannen."

Though I was shocked at first, it didn't take long for me to realize the logic behind his thinking. It was the raw emotion behind his response that got my attention. He was, after all, only insisting that I consider the people who needed me every day, and realize the value of that duty. I was a thirty-one-year-old mother of three kids under the age of 11. I had no right to take myself away from them or Randy. But I was looking for a way to vent my anger and desperation over everything that happened since 9/11. I was looking for a way to channel my outrage. Randy couldn't see the depth of my passion or understand how 9/11 had affected me.

Little did I know, the path I was seeking would present itself soon.

Shortly after the invasion of Afghanistan, I saw a television commercial advertising American car flags. I reached for the cordless phone and bought them then and there. I remember how happy I was when they arrived. Included were two window decals of Old Glory, two car flags, and a small but beautiful 9/11 commemorative pin. I immediately put the window decals on the front and back doors of our home, the commemorative pin on my winter coat, and rolled down the back windows of my car and attached the two car flags. I felt such a sense of pride. This was one of my ways of showing support for our military fighting the forces of evil over in Afghanistan and displaying my newfound love for my country following 9/11. When it came time to reorder checks for our checking account, I found a website that offered checks depicting the scene of the firefighters at Ground Zero holding up the American flag—much like the image of the World War II Marines who fought to save our flag on the shores of Iwo Jima. My new checks would arrive bearing the motto "9/11: We will never forget."

I was outraged when our political leaders encouraged us to resume life as normal. "Go shopping," they said. "Take a trip!" I clearly remember thinking that the fires that burned at Ground Zero for more than three months had only recently been put out, we are at war, we had lost nearly three thousand lives on that tragic day, and my government wanted me to just go shopping or take a trip! It felt like a slap in the face of our grieving country, those 9/11 families who would never have their loved ones come home ever again, and those families whose loved ones were risking their lives to fight a war far away in a world we didn't understand. I felt very strongly that as long as the al-Qaeda threat remained, life could not, and should not, return to what it was before the attacks. Each of us had a responsibility to aid the nation's response to the crisis to the best of our abilities. Doing otherwise would mean failing to honor those who died, and those who lost them.

Al-Qaeda and bin Laden were on my mind every day, and I resolved back then that I would not rest until the evil man behind the 9/11 attacks was dead or in custody. My resolve remains the same today.

Eventually I turned to our family computer in my quest to deal with everything I was feeling. I opened up Yahoo and started to read. One night I came across one of the many video memorials being circulated on the Internet related to the 9/11 tragedy. It was set to a song called "Can't Cry Hard Enough." I thought it was the most moving and harrowing tribute. "Can't cry hard enough" essentially became my mantra and a regular reminder of the loss and the duty we owe to those who die. I have listened to and viewed this memorial more times than I can count, and every time my emotions get the best of me.

One evening after work while I was flipping between the cable news channels, caught up in the aftermath of the anthrax attacks, the still-burning rubble at Ground Zero, and the just-commenced Operation Enduring Freedom going on in Afghanistan, I caught a news report about how Internet chat rooms and forums were being used as communication venues for terrorist groups such as al-Qaeda and their supporters. I wrote down the URL of the website mentioned in the news report. The site alneda.com (*alneda* means "the truth") was a popular site before and after the 9/11 attacks. Back then these terrorist Internet sites weren't password protected. You could log on to them as you could to any news site. Not long after I read the news report on alneda.com, it was gone. So I searched for others like it, and soon discovered terrorist forums such as the Castleforum, Arabforum, and Repairforum. These seemed to be the most popular and radical of the bunch. The cool thing about such Internet forums is that you can link from one site to another, downloading files and videos—following a seemingly never-ending path within the dark world of the jihad communities. I trolled through, having no real idea of what the interaction and content meant. I couldn't read their language, Arabic. But I was mesmerized by the plethora of pictures of streets littered with glass and rubble and pieces of human flesh—celebrations of death, destruction, and mayhem. I also found gory videos primarily related to Hamas and suicide bombings. This shadowy world I was discovering couldn't have been further from my own, and I felt the intrigue festering inside me. Widespread interest in Afghanistan, the Taliban, and al-Qaeda was really just beginning then, and I would soon see a flood of support for the jihadists erupting in the forums centered around anti-American, anti-Western fervor.

But I was frustrated that I couldn't understand what was being discussed. In an effort to change this, I began to search for software translation programs or other resources that would allow me to see the Arabic dialogue in English. Overcome with curiosity, I spent $565 to download one of the more highly recommended programs available at the time.

The pictures and videos on the sites were so clear that I could almost guess their locations. But they didn't scare me, just as I wasn't scared of the beheading videos that would eventually become so popular. I wasn't going to let them stop me.

A drawback of machine translation software is that you don't get the whole context, just an idea of what's being said. It's not necessarily reliable for drawing larger conclusions. The first night I could read the chatter, I thought, "Is this for real?" I observed it for weeks. I would keep track of the forums that I thought were particularly prolific. I wanted to know if these guys had any salt. Then I started hearing some television news reports that followed or related to what they were talking about. Television and online news sites became my barometer for gauging the truth and veracity of what went on inside the terrorist sites, further fueling my determination. With my growing desire to understand what was actually taking place in these terrorist Internet sites, I decided I wanted to interact.

In early 2002, I signed up for online Arabic courses from the Cairo-based Sa'nna Online Academy. I could work on the lessons on my own time and pace. The first part is training your mind to read from right to left, and understanding the differences in structure between Arabic and English. In Arabic there are two types of sentences—nominal and verbal. Nominal sentences contain a subject and a predicate, and the verb must agree with the subject in number and gender. Whereas a verbal sentence begins with a verb and contains at least a verb and subject, with the verb always in the singular form, even for the cases where the subject is plural. So understanding Arabic grammar didn't come naturally to me. I really had to focus. I completed those twelve lessons as soon as I could manage. Through these online lessons, I found the Al-Kitaab beginner learning textbooks, and started practicing writing. I learned to construct simple phrases and sentences following the examples provided, as excited as if I were a child again, learning to read and write. My goal was to truly communicate in these forums, maybe even starting up dialogues with al-Qaeda members and supporters.

The first thing I ever posted was "Death to America." It was March 13, 2002. Others repeated the saying, so I knew I was on the right track. The jihadi cheerleaders in the forums usually chime in after someone has posted something of value by simply commenting, "Praise be to you . . . Praise be to Allah . . . Honor to you for bringing this issue." And then "Death to America! Death to America! Death to the West! Death to Israel!" I had to start somewhere, and my monitoring of the dynamics of these sites told me jihadi cheerleading was my best bet.

My copy of the Koran is now worn and dog-eared from constant use. I have studied it closely, searching for the passages that will resonate. I am careful to never be too perfect in my grammar and spelling. I make those errors that, from years of watching and reading what they say, I know a "brother" would make. Still, I worry.

When I made my first appearance in the forums as a young radical Muslim looking to find my way to jihad, I called myself Abu Hamdi—without a clear sense of who that was. I decided he should begin as a bumbling naïf, a lost soul searching for acceptance and a path away from the diaspora existence he hated.

I began quietly posting simple phrases asking the wise brothers of the mujahideen for guidance and direction. I did not garner much attention early on, but that served me well. By all appearances, I was one of them—a supporter of the mujahideen and my Muslim brothers; an able and willing young man seeking to do his duty for the cause of jihad. As I grew more comfortable in the skin of Abu Hamdi, I interacted more with the other members in the Internet forums. I remember finding a website that had posted the instructions for the "last night of life," written by 9/11 lead hijacker Mohammad Atta, that contained Islamic prayers and a practical checklist of reminders for the final operation. The "Atta letter" also referenced two of the traditional chapters of the Koran related to war and martyrdom, al-Tawba and Anfal. I decided that this would be good material to post in the Internet forums asking for wisdom and understanding. It worked well. The leaders of the forums responded immediately.

From then on, I tried to always have a couple of identities active and participating so that if I screwed up with one I could still have another to work with. In my early days in the jihadi forums, I used various tactics and methods to mask or hide my true IP (Internet protocol) address. I knew that a computer user could easily be tracked down or located by simply tracing the IP address associated with a computer, and I did not want any of my newfound friends getting curious about where I was located.

In the process of my online evolution as a radicalized Muslim holy warrior supporting the cause of jihad and al-Qaeda, I spent thousands of hours infiltrating terrorist websites and chat rooms. I would eventually create over three dozen identities. Some were real doozies. I built my false identities into characters with personal histories and contacts that had specific skill sets and talents. They had backgrounds appropriate to their purported locations, as well as the proper ties to various tribes or clans. Early on, I learned that cultural respect and honor was a constant that I would need to incorporate into how I operated my undercover identities. Each character's narrative was like its own novella. One guy ran a network of couriers. Another was a wealthy businessman eager to finance jihad. Except for the few I made into inexperienced and wayward souls looking for guidance, all of my characters were strong personalities whose dominance would be accepted and valued in the online jihadi community.

I was very careful and systematic, tracking names and contacts with an Excel spreadsheet and copying conversations with screen shots that certified the time and date of the posts and communications from these radicals. It became painfully clear how effective these sites were in creating an environment where impressionable and disaffected Muslims or any susceptible individual could be easily indoctrinated, radicalized, and trained for the cause of jihad.

After the U.S. and coalition forces invaded Afghanistan and destroyed the al-Qaeda training camps, rather than being defeated by the lack of viable training locations, al-Qaeda and its support base displayed one of their hallmark strengths—creativity—by establishing online training camps and introducing the popular *Jihad Encyclopedia and Training Manual,* allowing individuals to self-train as mujahideen to participate in jihad. Soon, this spawned the phenomenon of self-trained splinter groups that could simply associate themselves with and pledge an oath to al-Qaeda to become mujahideen—a far more efficient process than the traditional routes would-be jihadists had to take prior to 9/11.

Early on, I noticed that a lot of the behavioral characteristics displayed by individuals in the jihadi sites recalled those of the garden-variety criminals, serial killers, and deviants I had studied for most of my life. But there was one significant difference—the importance of Arab culture and Islam. In Arab culture, there is such a strong tribal or clan association, and the survival mentality dictates how the society functions, with significant variations across regions and countries. These intricate details would prove critical to my success in operating my jihadi identities online.

CHAPTER THREE

CYBER SPY

In November 2002, as the Bush administration was pushing hard for intervention in Iraq, I remember watching U.S. Secretary of State Colin Powell testify before the United Nations, making the case for military intervention and incursion. As I sat watching Secretary Powell's UN testimony, I was aghast—failing to understand the logic for the administration's position on Iraq as well as the impending immediacy for action against the Saddam Hussein regime. I clearly remember thinking, "What the hell? We're not even done in Afghanistan." The allegations about Iraq's WMD program laid the groundwork for a military cause much larger and more significant than what we had witnessed with the invasion of Afghanistan. At each stage leading up to the Iraqi conflict, I would simply ask "Why?" The reasoning for the U.S. and a coalition of international forces invading Iraq never added up to me.

Right after 9/11, I was incredibly frustrated, wondering why we weren't doing anything. But the quagmire we went on to create in Iraq was a shameful reaction. I'm not a Democrat, and I'm not Republican.

I will support the military and I support the troops because they're the ones being sent to the front lines to fight. The Kurds, the Shiites, and the Sunnis have never gotten along. How can we in the West impose our version of what we believe is democracy on a society whose culture is not designed for it? With all of the knowledge, experience, and understanding I have gained since 9/11, it's clear to me that the clash of cultures and civilizations that has been waxing and waning for centuries will not be resolved in my lifetime—and certainly not by American military force.

In the terrorist forums and on their sites, I'm only pretending to be anti-American, anti-Western, anti-Zionist, but frankly, when we invaded Iraq, I believe we gave the people of Iraq every reason in the world to hate us. By occupying Muslim lands, we legitimized all of their decades-old complaints. The war in Iraq will always be a mistake, and I don't think there is anything that we can do to make it right. What we can and should do is step back and acknowledge the important differences between the U.S. and Iraqi worlds, develop respect for their culture, and work to find common ground so we can diminish and defeat the terrorism that is a threat to both of our societies.

At first, in the forums, I was feeling my way around gingerly. Now I know the tribes and their nuances so well that I could probably whip out a new identity within ten minutes.

When I need to post pictures of my guys (my online personas), I collect different photographs of individuals who are Arab-looking, if not ethnically Middle Eastern. If I need to change things, I can photoshop them. Today I get some of them from Arabic groups on social networking sites such as Facebook. Of course, in these cases, I have to manipulate the photo somewhat. Sometimes I'll blur the face a little. I would never pick a picture that was planted all over the place. I even find a lot of pictures in local blogs in that part of the world. And I get many from travel sites and travel blogs. Sometimes it's just Mustafa from the local falafel shop.

When we went to war in Iraq, I had never paid attention to what kind of planes, ammunition, or helicopters our country had. I didn't even know what a Black Hawk was. But once I started learning about it, I found myself loving the whole culture. My favorite of the military planes was the A-10 Warthog Tankbuster, known as a tank killer, one of the planes that had served the Air Force well back in the first Gulf War. The Tankbuster has one of the largest, heaviest, and most powerful guns in the U.S. air fleet. The gun is a GAU-8/A Avenger with a 30mm, seven-barrel Gatling gun capable of delivering four thousand shots per minute. I loved the thought of the Tankbuster flying over the skies of Afghanistan and Iraq, taking out Taliban and al-Qaeda fighters and Iraqi insurgents.

At the start of the Afghan war, there were several descriptions of the different bombs in the U.S. military arsenal. My favorite was the mammoth Daisy Cutter, which is the fifteen-thousand-pound conventional bomb usually delivered by a C-130 transport. I remember watching one of the videos released by the Pentagon of the Daisy Cutter after it was dropped over Afghanistan following a reported bin Laden sighting. The bomb's deployment and detonation was an awesome show of force, and the level of destruction revealed in its aftermath should have been enough to demonstrate the mighty power of the U.S. military to al-Qaeda and the Taliban.

People can't believe it when I tell them I've never been to Pakistan or Afghanistan. It's thanks to the Internet that I've taught myself so much about these countries' cultures, and I can design my online personas so that they are as realistic as any flesh and blood individual.

Of course, the wonderful democracy of the Internet also comes with a dark side. It was a boon to the terrorist groups and their supporters well in advance of 9/11. They have used the Internet to master and advance their objectives far more efficiently and effectively than have the governments of the U.S. and most other countries. I learned this from my targets early on. By following their lead, I honed my own proficiency with the Internet and all of its vast resources—ultimately using what they had taught me against them.

A COMPUTER SCREEN, SHINING OUT through the dark of night, makes me feel safe. With my fingers on the keyboard, I am in control, selecting words and concepts, erasing those I don't want. It's perfect until I move the mouse arrow to the tiny box labeled "send." Suddenly, it's not so safe.

Once I click send in an email, I've opened a door. Even when I have checked and rechecked the content and context of my message, and the security sending protocols I put into place before any email message is ever sent out, I always hesitate. I have to stay vigilant, lest I set myself up for failure. If I have garbled the syntax or somehow miscalculated the meaning of a scripture from the Koran, I may scare my mark or invite questions about who I am.

In late October of 2003, on the cusp of autumn, the air is cold and tight and the wind can be harsh, always signaling the preamble to winter in northwestern Montana. Conrad rests in a valley, which thankfully provides some protection for the fierce Montana winds that blow through the prairie. Still, I can hear the tiny pings of wet, icy snowflakes on the windowpane already.

My early-morning routine is becoming comfortably familiar. I wake up at my usual time, 4:00, and quietly pad down to the computer, popping open a Diet Coke and logging on. This morning, I'm greeted by one of my favorite Todd Rundgren songs, "Hello, It's Me."

I start the day like most Americans do, by reading the news. But instead of the local Montana paper, I read the news from around the world, especially the Middle East. I have my favorite international news outlets that I visit every day, such as the BBC, the *Washington Post, Jerusalem Post, Jordan Daily, Yemen Times,* ArabNews Online, the Saudi Press Agency, and many other U.S. dailies.

As usual, I am looking for news of the Middle East, mostly from foreign newspapers and news services, who view events in Iraq differently than we do in the U.S. Not correctly, necessarily, but differently. This is what I want and need—interpretation of world events from outlets not influenced and published by Western or U.S. interests.

Today's headline is about this year's Nobel Prize winners. I skim that story quickly, then search for the news that my Internet "comrades" would find most interesting.

In the *Jerusalem Post,* I scan a story on how Palestinians have "condemned" a $5 million reward offered by the U.S. for information about a Gaza Strip attack of an American convoy on October 15, 2003. Col. Rashid Abu Shabak, commander of the Palestinian Authority's Preventive Security Service, calls the announcement insulting "because it deals with a people whose worth does not waver in the face of financial temptations." Another official dubs the U.S. reward "a stab in the back of the Palestinians, who are doing their utmost to capture the culprits." I save this story, transferring it to my Palestinian notebook, knowing it could surface in one of my online conversations that day or even the next week.

Even though I have been at this for many years, I am still haunted by the vehement hatred the jihadists feel for the U.S. In my next dialogue with a Palestinian contact, I will register my own outrage over the reward. This will help me keep his trust and possibly learn his secrets.

I take note of another story, this one in the *Washington Post* that details how the Pakistani city of Quetta is becoming the "new headquarters of the extremist Taliban movement." The article quotes a Pakistani journalist who claims, "Thousands of Taliban fighters reside in mosques and madrassas with the full support of a provincial ruling party and militant Pakistani groups. Taliban leaders wanted by the U.S. and Kabul governments are living openly in nearby villages." I flag this article as well, primarily because it is further confirmation of what I have been hearing from my own contacts in Pakistan.

The news reports are all pieces of the puzzle; snippets of information that help me judge what is truth from what is fiction. I could spend hours searching the world news, but I have emails to send, so I log on, instead, to one of my many email sites.

The email account that I had created for my newly developed identity, Abu Latif, had a few new messages waiting to be opened. As I opened up the first email, which contained an attachment, all of a sudden everything on my screen faded to black. Apparently, one of my jihadist "friends" had sent me a virus embedded in the image file.

Though we had other computers networked and running in our home at the time, the computer I was using that morning was the main machine. Randy and I had shared the same workstation for years, with separate log-ins, and it had worked fine. Generally, when I was doing what I do, no one was home, awake, or paying too much attention, so we had no reason to want separate computers. That is, until today!

I began to panic, trying everything to get the machine running. Nothing worked. I couldn't even get a power surge going. I was going to have to wait for Randy to wake up in another two and a half hours. The prospect of that much idle time made my panic rise again.

Finally, I resolved to stop trying to fix things I didn't even understand, lest I make it worse. At the moment, I was only preoccupied with my own worries about the dead computer; I hadn't even considered the fact that Randy's business records and other important information were in there too. All I cared about was getting back online and making sure I had not lost any of the documents and materials I had been compiling in my double life.

As the time passed, excruciatingly slowly, I kept thinking, "What the hell am I going to tell Randy?" He had no clue what I was doing on the computer. He just knew that I was interested in al-Qaeda and the War on Terror. When he finally got out of bed, I simply told him, "I don't know what happened, but I went to turn on the computer and it won't turn on." He's got to have coffee before he does anything, so he brushed me off momentarily and went to sit in the kitchen. Still panicking, I followed him all over the house, even to the bathroom, until he asked, "*What* is up with you this morning?"

I said, "Could you just try and get the computer to go on?"

"What the hell?" he replied. "What do you need?"

"Well, I *really* need to get these things done before these trials I have coming up. I had planned my time this morning to do it."

He said, "Jesus, Shannen . . . everything was working fine with the computer as of last night!"

I decided that nothing would be resolved that morning, and headed to work. When I came home for lunch, Randy was working on the computer and growling. He looked puzzled and annoyed—I didn't pick at him, knowing it would just aggravate him. When I got home that night, I kept a safe distance, busying myself with getting dinner started and helping the kids with their homework. Finally, just before dinner was ready, Randy emerged from the office with a stormy look on his face.

He now had the computer up and running, and he said, "Do you want to tell me what *really* happened?"

I explained, "I opened up an email and something was attached to it. Then it went black."

"I know," Randy replied. "But why in the world is there this strange language all over and in your emails? If you want this stuff back, you're going to have to tell me what it all is." Clearly, my story about needing these computer files for upcoming trials was not going to wash.

Some of the files Randy had recovered included Arabic file names, and he demanded to know what I was doing. I said, "I told you what happened, and that's really what happened. Sometimes I find things on the Internet that are interesting, and I like to save them."

He grabbed the computer's mouse and threw it against the wall, where I watched it break into pieces.

Then he went to the garage for a long time. When he came back, he said, "I'm not going to have you anywhere near my computer, if that's what you're doing." He put together my own computer for me to work on. And our space became like two different offices in one. You could have put a piece of tape down the middle of the floor to divide up the sides. Randy had his half and I had mine. I had Osama toilet paper on my side, which says "wipe here," and a leprechaun on top of my computer monitor that represents my Irish heritage and my stubborn spirit. I surrounded my desk with a Betsy Ross commemorative plate, inspirational quotes, World War I and II posters, and a framed picture of Rick Springfield—my obsession for over twenty years. I loved that nobody would ever find anything out about my work again.

If only.

In the virtual world of Internet forums, you develop your own clique of friends much as you would in the real world. In July of 2002,

I discovered a guy based outside of Karachi, a Jordanian who kept entering our little circle claiming he had Stinger missiles. At the time, I was trying to figure out how to be a leader in the forums. As an experiment, I wrote to him, "You are an infidel undercover. You have no missiles." The guy repeated his claim that he got them from a source in Pakistan. He said he had access to these missiles and for the right price I could get them to the people who needed them. I still didn't believe him, and I didn't want him to be a distraction, so I started to challenge his honor, which is a common tactic within the jihadist culture. I kept trying to push him away and make him look like a fool in the forum. Then he posted these two pictures of him sitting on crates, which he claimed contained the missiles.

There were stock numbers visible on the crates, even though the picture wasn't great. So I wrote, "So you have the boxes. There's nothing in there." Then he posted pictures of the contents. Now I was nervous, as well as pissed off that he was distracting me from my ambition to become a leader of this forum. So for four or five days I thought, "What do I do with this?" I had no way to determine if the pictures were legitimate or not. Stock numbers and the email correspondence in hand, I first intended to drive to the closest field office for the FBI here in Montana, but was afraid the FBI would not take me seriously. What were the chances of a Montana mom showing up at their door with information about an individual who was trying to sell Stinger missiles?

In the end, I went to the FBI tip line and submitted everything. I didn't want to contact the local police because Conrad is a small town and I didn't want people to wonder what I was doing. I gave my name and told them that I wasn't a quack, that I am a legitimate person; here's the number to my court chambers. I thought that was the end of it. I figured they could check me out, and see that I was a judge and not a wacko. I just wanted them to look at it. But that didn't happen.

What did happen was that Gail, my clerk, came in one day when I was in a hearing, so I called a break. Gail said, "There's this guy who says he's from the FBI Joint Terrorism Task Force from New Jersey. He's got to talk to you right now!"

"Tell him I'll call him back. I'm not breaking court for that!" I can't imagine what Gail thought, but I was annoyed. Wasn't a tip line just that? What was up with this phone call?

After my hearings that day I called the guy back, thinking he wouldn't be in the office at 6:30 and I could leave him a voice message. He called back again the next day and left a message. I decided I'd call him from my cell phone out in the parking lot.

He said, "Why did you contact the FBI and submit these materials?"

"I had no way to determine whether this was legitimate or not," I whispered hesitatingly, hoping no one would see me and come knock on my window. I felt like Deep Throat. I clearly had no idea what I was getting myself into.

"Why do you even have this information?" He asked as if he were interrogating me.

I explained things as they happened, and tried to leave it at that. I said that after 9/11 I got interested in the Middle East and terrorist culture, so I started to go to certain extremist websites to observe and monitor information and materials in the sites and the interaction and communications of site members. I had submitted the guy's email address and associated IP address, the link to the Internet site containing his forum profile and posts, as well as the two digital photos of the crates containing the Stinger missiles.

When I thought about it from his perspective, I could understand why he was dubious. I answered enough questions to satisfy him, and then I didn't hear from him for a while. But one day Gail came into court again and said, "It's that guy from New Jersey. He's really pushy." I decided to take the call, but I was irked. I said, "Why are you calling the court when I gave you my cell phone number?"

He apologized. "We were able to prove those were stock inventory weapons that were provided to the mujahideen, and beyond that I can't give you any more specific information."

I took him at his word. As would become my practice with almost all such tips I would eventually provide to the FBI, once I knew my part was done I rarely asked, "What happened with that case?" Handing things over is my closure.

AROUND THIS TIME, I WENT to Buffalo, New York, to take an intensive Arabic-language course. I had managed to get Randy's support to take vacation time to do this. Though I was excited, I felt some guilt about the time away from my family, especially my youngest daughter, who was almost seven at the time. She was into the Care Bears, and I had been looking everywhere for the Good Luck Care Bear, but hadn't been successful. The morning I left she asked me, with her big brown smiling eyes, to find Good Luck Bear and bring him home, and I said I would try my hardest. Needless to say, a visit to a local Toys R Us store in the Buffalo area effortlessly yielded the Good Luck Bear, much to my daughter's delight.

Close to Buffalo is the city of Lackawanna, New York, a poor, old industrial city that has a strong, mostly Yemeni, Muslim community. In Montana, we don't have a Muslim population. So this experience would be my first real-life encounter with the culture and people of a Muslim community. I was excited, to say the least. I was also interested in visiting Lackawanna because the city had been in the news for the so-called "Lackawanna Six," a group of al-Qaeda members that had been convicted of providing material support to al-Qaeda. I was also intrigued by the Masjid Alhuda Guidance Mosque, the largest in the Buffalo area. I parked my rental car nearby and walked the streets, completely thrilled to be there, immersed in it. I saw women in the traditional headscarves and imagined for myself what their lives must be like, how different from mine—even though we shared the U.S. as our home. This was my first chance to see what Muslim bookstores were like. I had learned online that you could buy jihadist videos, recruiting and training videos, but I wasn't going to push it with the owner, who was kind to me. I just wanted to experience the whole thing without being noticed too much, except for the fact that I was the lone blond woman walking the streets.

I went back the next day to soak it in even more. Everywhere I went I was met with nothing but warmth and friendliness. One shopkeeper took me to the mosque and introduced me to the local Imam. I felt the positive aspects of Islam most keenly when the people in Lackawanna proudly showed me a beautiful soccer field they had built for their kids. It was a green oasis in a world of dirty brick.

The language course would help discipline me that much more toward what I was doing on the computer. While in Buffalo, I also took some time to visit Niagara Falls and was fascinated with the legendary falls and the *Maid of the Mist*. In addition to picking up Good Luck Bear, I also bought some Niagara Falls and *Maid of the Mist* trinkets to bring home to the family.

CHAPTER FOUR

A CALL TO JIHAD

In late 2002, I found my way to an Internet forum called itshappening.com, for individuals like myself who were interested in following terrorist threats online. I began interacting and working with a small group at the forum. It was a great venue for those of us seeking to follow the War on Terror, to engage and interact with each other.

The identity that I created for myself at itshappening.com was as "luvlaw1."

I gradually became comfortable with how the forum members posted and analyzed their "finds" from the jihadist sites, and I began the process of introducing myself to their fold. I eventually decided to participate in discussions regarding information posted and analyzed from the jihadist sites. At first, it was an overwhelming experience, since all my previous Internet sleuthing had been solo. Though I read the public discussions in some of the sites, I had refrained from interacting as myself in any discussion forums before.

Itshappening.com had members from Australia, Canada, the U.S., and Singapore. The members that appeared to have the most knowledge and grasp of the information and materials in the jihadist sites used screen names such as "rogue," "hammy," "n," "casey," "sacha," "bushido," "katie," "peg," "John," and "asp." This handful of members appeared to interact in its own group, and the forum member known as "Rogue" appeared to be leading this group. I eventually started posting information from the forums that related to the things they were discussing and analyzing, and that quickly got their attention. My perspective seemed to mesh well with their collective mindset. Rogue eventually asked me to join their tight-knit group, inviting me to a private MSN discussion group, separate from their public presence at itshappening.com. We became a loosely associated bunch calling ourselves the Seven Seas Global Intelligence Group (7Seas).

As we formalized our association, our goal was to become a private intelligence company with the objective of securing some private funding or government contracts to expand our efforts in fighting terrorism. But this turned out to be much more difficult than we expected. Almost everyone in the group had a day job and devoted any extra time they had to our collective passion of fighting terrorism.

Our efforts continued until January 2004, when I would leave the group in the fallout of a high-profile case I was involved in. I decided to proceed with my Internet work on a solo basis.

WHEN I FIRST BEGAN COLLABORATING and working with the people of 7Seas, I continued to work privately within the jihadist forums, keeping the majority of my work close to the vest. I appreciated the interaction and collaboration with others, but I wasn't nearly ready to reveal the extent of who I was and what I was doing on my own.

When I first ventured into the jihadist forums, I noticed that certain forum participants were leaders with many followers and tight control of their flock. So it became my practice to take control and rule with an iron fist while working my online characters, a tactic that gained me respect and a following which to this day draws in new blood. When focusing on a new individual, I work them to essentially pledge an oath (*bayat*) to my character and whatever terrorist group and ideology I purport to extol. In advancing my undercover characters in the jihadist forums, I always give the appearance of a security-conscious and paranoid leader who distrusts my subjects until they prove their worth in my eyes. It is in this context that I began my pursuit of Oussama Abdullah Kassir, in my efforts to infiltrate his lair and that of his jihad media organization, the Islamic Media Front.

In late 2002, I began following one of the more well-known online jihadists who used the online name of "Abu Khadija" and the email address khadija1417@hotmail.com. Abu Khadija, whose real name was Oussama Abdullah Kassir, is a Swedish citizen of Lebanese descent with a long history of involvement in both real-world and Internet terrorist activities. Kassir was known to have deep roots and ties to Algeria's Armed Islamic Group going back the mid-1990s.

On the Internet front, Kassir was known to be the force behind the Islamic Media Center (IMC). The IMC was one of the early online groups to pioneer jihadist media and propaganda. Kassir was also responsible for authoring the *Poison Handbook and Explosives Manual* of the *Mujahideen Terrorist Handbook*. Although I didn't know it at the time, Kassir would later be indicted in the Federal District Court of the Southern District of New York for his participation with Abu Hamza al-Masri, the "Hook Sheik" and radical London cleric from the Finsbury Park Mosque, in their conspiracy to set up a terrorist training camp in Bly, Oregon, in 1999 and 2000. Prior to being accused of conspiring to set up the Bly training camp, Abu Hamza al-Masri was best known for his radical Islamic teachings and support for terrorist activities, which he regularly conducted out of the mosque. This mosque was, by then, a well-known breeding ground for radical Islamist views. Among the notorious former Mosque attendees were "shoe bomber" Richard Reid and alleged twentieth hijacker Zacarias Moussaoui. Kassir was also known to have trained in al-Qaeda's Darunta training camp in Afghanistan in the late 1990s. Because I am a woman and could never infiltrate the realm of al-Qaeda in the real world, I was that much more determined to infiltrate them online, and Kassir presented a viable target for this purpose.

When I first made contact with Kassir online in early 2003, he was still an active public persona. It was only when the *Jihad Encyclopedia* and *Mujahideen Terrorist Handbook* came out, to which he contributed, and his association with Abu Hamza became public knowledge, that he went underground—ultimately disappearing from the online jihadist community in late 2004. I began my courtship of Kassir by working to obtain his trust, with the goal of sharing an email account where we could "safely" leave messages for each other in the draft file, avoiding the chance that any of our messages could be intercepted by the infidel oppressors. This was a tactic that I established early on to gain the trust of my Internet targets. I gave them a "sense of security" by advising that we could safely communicate by leaving messages in the draft folders of email accounts. This was an incredibly efficient way to obtain valuable information I could subsequently provide to the authorities to head off any developing threats.

Because Kassir was a well-known jihadist with real ties to al-Qaeda, I was careful and specific in how I approached him. The role I chose was that of a recruiter for a newly formed group of mujahideen located in Canada. I had created an identity I called Abu Zeida, who I then worked to establish as one of my main online characters.

I chose Canada because one of my close associates from 7Seas was from Canada, so I had someone familiar with the area I was purporting to be operating from.

After exchanging emails and materials back and forth over a period of months, and showing off my "jihadist prowess" in the forums, I took the chance of asking Kassir if he was interested in discussing important and sensitive information about how we might be able to work together to further the cause of our fighting brothers in Afghanistan and Chechnya. Thankfully, he replied that he was interested and inquired how we should proceed to discreetly communicate. BOOM! I was in! Though I suggested my draft file idea, I hardly expected he would offer up his email address and password—but when he did, there was no way in hell I was going to argue.

Once inside, however, I was always careful to mark emails that I had opened as unread, giving all appearances of not disturbing the contents of his account. Of course, I was copying all his contacts and other materials in the account I believed were valuable.

In the meantime, I was collaborating more with my 7Seas associates. In early 2003, we were all covering various threats leading up to the invasion of Iraq in March of that year. There were plenty of interesting materials being passed around and posted in the jihadist forums. One threat-related string told of al-Qaeda perfecting the use of cell phones to simultaneously detonate remote car bombs. Toward the end of the month, I was able to obtain the schematics for the perfected cell phone bomb detonators. Al-Qaeda was bragging about this simple but highly effective terrorist weapon, and it was now determining the perfect venue to highlight it. This threat became my top priority.

Throughout the next month, it became clear that the targets being selected for the next big "hit" by al-Qaeda were Western interests in the Saudi Kingdom, and the method would be the use of the cell phones to simultaneously detonate car bombs.

On March 20, 2003, the U.S. and a coalition of international forces—similar to the coalition of forces that participated in the invasion and military action in Afghanistan—commenced its invasion of Iraq through the territory of coalition partner Kuwait.

In building the case for intervention in Iraq, the U.S. had stated that its intent was to remove the Saddam Hussein regime because it was actively working to develop weapons of mass destruction, it supported and facilitated terrorism, had committed devastating human rights violations against its people, and routinely snubbed its nose at the world community by defying the authority and demands of the United Nations. To support its position of regime change in Iraq, the U.S. and U.K. relied on the authority of UN Security Council Resolutions 678 and 687 to use all necessary means to compel Iraq to comply with its international obligations.

Through the efforts of the U.S. and U.K., and the support of the members of the UN Security Council, Resolution 1441 was unanimously adopted on November 8, 2002, providing Iraq with one last opportunity to comply with the Security Council Resolutions mandating disarmament or face the consequences of military actions to force compliance. Resolution 1441 strengthened the mandate of the UN Monitoring and Verification Commission (UNMOVIC) and the International Atomic Energy Agency (IAEA) arms of the Security Council to allow inspectors to reenter Iraq to investigate at will and verify the process of disarmament.

With the U.S. and coalition forces invading Iraq in March of 2003, al-Qaeda had been handed a new platform to further rally its support base and expand its growing influence in the Arab world. Though the organization had previously coordinated car bombings to occur simultaneously in different locations—a hallmark practice of the terrorist organization—it had not previously been able to implement and perfect the use of cell phones as remote detonators.

Throughout March and May of 2003, my 7Seas partners and I assiduously analyzed all of the information and communications that had been collected from the jihadist Internet sites and put together a solid intel package to submit to the FBI in hopes of heading off al-Qaeda's next big attack, which we all knew would be coming soon.

By May 8, 2003, the package was ready to go. It contained enough information on the kind of attack that was planned, the general location, and that the attack would be carried out by the use of cell phones as remote bomb detonators. We had concluded that the coming attack would target Western interests in the Saudi kingdom—most likely in Riyadh.

In the course of my years in the jihadist forums, I had come to learn that when terrorist chatter goes quiet, it usually means that an attack has moved from the planning to the execution phase. Though at times they have done this as a purposeful diversion, it is more often a big red flag. In the first days of May 2003, the jihadist forums went dark and the traffic slowed. My 7Seas colleagues and I could only hope that the information and materials we had submitted in the intel package had been received and routed to the authorities in time to prevent what al-Qaeda was planning.

Then, al-Qaeda struck with a vengeance.

The afternoon of May 12, I had just gotten home from work and sat down at my computer to check in with my 7Seas friends when the news broke that there had been a series of car bombs in Riyadh. The horrific details of death and destruction of the attack would be reported throughout the night.

The terrorist group had successfully detonated four car bombs simultaneously in the Saudi Kingdom, targeting Western housing complexes. Thirty-four people were killed—including eight Americans—and 160 were injured. Americans, Westerners, and non-Saudis were all targeted in the Kingdom.

I was stunned, as were my 7Seas colleagues. We were not only mad but devastated. And I still had to attend to my duties as a wife and mother before I could find the time that evening to start following the news and Internet forums for nuggets of information on the bombings. I remember rushing through dinner that night and checking the status of the kids' homework and talking with Randy about my day. Since the time of the computer crash the year before, Randy had been aware that I was acting in a more operational context in the jihadist Internet forums. Even though he had an idea of what I was doing online, I still fiercely protected the details of exactly what I was doing. I knew I was walking a fine line, but I was confident in my ability to prevent my virtual life online from wreaking havoc in my real life.

Four days after the Riyadh bombings, on May 16, al-Qaeda struck again in Casablanca, killing forty-five and injuring scores more. Five explosions targeted a Jewish community center, a Spanish restaurant and social club, a hotel, and the Belgian consulate.

If I had had a more formalized relationship with the FBI at that time, I could have screamed, "What the hell happened?" I reasoned that enough information had been submitted to have prevented the attack, had the right people been paying attention.

Back in 2003, however, there wasn't the deluge of car bombings we eventually saw materialize during the Iraq war. Up to that time, car bombings had been the hallmark of terrorist groups like the IRA,

Hamas, and Hezbollah. The Riyadh and Casablanca bombings signaled a shift—they were the debut performance of al-Qaeda's newly perfected bombing technique, which it would go on to use often.

Though the intelligence and law enforcement authorities, not only here in the U.S. but in their partner countries, could have connected the dots and heightened awareness of an impending attack, they didn't. I have always felt that we (7Seas) could not have been the only people in the U.S. or other parts of the world that were aware of what was coming. Though the information and intel package that had been submitted on May 8 was not detailed and specific enough to name the Western housing complexes in Riyadh that were targeted, it certainly communicated that Western interests in the Saudi Kingdom were the likely targets.

As disappointed as I was at the loss of lives in Riyadh and Casablanca, it only hardened my resolve. The same was true for my colleagues at 7Seas.

Later on in 2003, I began following more closely one of the more popular and prolific online jihadists, known as Abu Banan, who was associated with the Global Islamic Media Group—another jihadist media and propaganda group that later merged with Kassir's IMC to become the Global Islamic Media Group (GIMG).

Back then, GIMG was the go-to venue for jihadist media and propaganda. (Later, al-Qaeda created the As-Sahab Foundation for Islamic Media Publication, which has since become its popular and effective media production arm.)

Prior to starting the GIMG, Abu Banan operated a site called guraba.com, a web and graphic design business with offices in Montreal and Istanbul that served as a front for disseminating GIMG materials.

Abu Banan was later identified as being Ayad Yolcu, a Turkish citizen, residing in Montreal. In connecting the online dots related to Yolcu, I discovered that his brother, Abdullah, had been linked to Ramzi Yousef, the mastermind of the 1993 World Trade Center attack and nephew of Khalid Sheikh Mohammed, the mastermind of the 9/11 attacks. In published materials made available after the conclusion of Yousef's prosecution and conviction for the 1993 WTC attack, I discovered that he placed calls to two locations in Istanbul more than ten times in the days prior to the bombing. The calls were traced, and had been placed from the house where Yousef had been staying in New York City to a house in Istanbul's Uskudar district where his brother Abdullah Yolcu resided, as well as to a textile company in the city of Aksaray, called Guraba Tekstil, that was run by Yolcu and two Saudi business partners. Having linked the Yolcu brothers to Ramzi Yousef—who had long-standing and well-known associations with al-Qaeda—my determination to ensnare Yolcu and work my way inside GIMG were cemented.

Throughout 2003, I continued my pursuit of Yolcu and my goal of slipping Abu Khadija, or khadija1417, into GIMG, which was a slow but careful process. In early May of that year, I created a spoof email account, khadija14l7@hotmail.com (where I substituted the last number "1" of the address with the lowercase letter "l," intending to have this email ID ready for some undetermined purpose down the line). Once I had gained Yolcu's trust, I employed my trusty tactic of suggesting leaving our messages in the draft folder of a shared email account. Accepting my proposal, Yolcu created the email account 1422Abukirkuly@guraba.com, where we proceeded to drop messages for each other.

After my departure from 7Seas, the group would dissolve, with the remaining members continuing in a group effort under the name of Phoenix Intelligence Group. My undercover work with Yolcu and GIMG would continue throughout 2003 into 2004. My goal was to become a "known" jihadist in their eyes, and for a long time I felt myself getting closer and closer. However, in May of 2004, my cover would be blown, and all of the work I had done came to a swift end.

CHAPTER FIVE

FINDING A TRAITOR

After almost three years on the hunt in the jihadist forums, I was getting pretty comfortable in the "virtual skins" of my terrorist alter egos.

While busy with my GIMG operation, and working on other threats developing in the jihadist sites with my 7Seas partners, I encountered another individual who would soon become very important. On October 6, 2003, he popped up in a Yahoo Arabic message board called "bravemuslims," calling himself Amir Abdul Rashid— "Al Muj"—and listing almujahadeen47@yahoo.com as his email address. What initially caught my eye about this person was that he posted messages in English on the predominantely Arabic message board. One day, this misfit appeared to be seeking contact with al-Qaeda. His message read (all spelling mistakes in original emails):

Brothers, I have attempted to write to you before but for some reason I was

unable. My name is Abdul Rashid, and I am a brother from the far side of the

world. I am comitted to the freedom and peace of m Muslim brothers and sisters

everywhere. Soon, very soon, I will have an oppertunity to take my own end of the struggle against those who would oppress us, to the next level. Inshallah I

shall be closer to some of you, and can enlist your aid upon my arrival. While I

cannot say more for right now, I would like to encourage any Brave Muslims to

contact me and begin a dialog. Allah's warriors are at hand.

Salaam,

Amir Abdul-Rashid.

"Al-Muj"

p.s. I have posted my photo under the photos section for anyone wishing

confirmation of who I am.

He was basically saying, "Hey . . . al-Qaeda . . . I am here . . . let's chat." I was puzzled and my curiosity was piqued. There were just enough red flags with his initial post at bravemuslims, and he had left enough identity markers for me to follow if I needed to. I decided to not make contact initially but instead to follow him first, which I did for a couple of weeks, watching the few messages he posted, which were mostly benign—quotes from Islamic materials; nothing of concern. Still, his odd presence nagged at me.

Rashid was not too clever. I easily determined he had taken no measures to cover his online tracks or mask his IP address—which, of course, allowed me to start checking him out. I began compiling the initial information I had found on Rashid and his email ID. However, on November 2, he posted a message that I knew I had to act on immediately, if only to save this naïf from himself or from making contact with anyone who actually could steer him down the path he professed to desire. Rashid's November 2 message stated:

Wa salaam alaaykum,

Just curious, would there be any chance a brother who might be on the wrong

side at the present, could join up . . . defect so to speak? I have been touched

by the will of Allah (swt) and see that I may be headed for a great mistake, and
I may wish to correct that error before any sin is committed, but I am affraid at I
will either be unable to contact any other brothers, or will be killed before I can
make contact.

Salaam,

Abdul-Rashid

I already knew Rashid was located in the U.S. because his IP
address traced to the Seattle area. I had not yet determined his true
identity, but he would be on my radar until I determined what his
intentions were and whether he presented a threat.

As a part of the process of dropping my jihadist nuggets in the
forums and sites, I spent a lot of time drafting different types of materials to post or send to individuals I found of interest. One effective
technique was the call to jihad. The call to jihad is an invitation to
Muslims to perform their duties against the infidels through holy war.
It has been, for me, a crucial tool to separate those who might have
actual information from those who are simply playing a role in the
terrorist propaganda war.

The day Rashid posted the message, I was monitoring the bravemuslims message board and saw it immediately. I wanted to grab him
before he went much further. Because he was posting in English, I
decided to send him an English version of my call to jihad. It read:

Dear brothers in Islam,

As Salaamu' Alaikum wa Rahmatullahi.

I hope this message will find all of you in good health.

I call my brothers to do your muslim duty with your brothers in jihad. And
verily I appeal by the nobles brothers we must train ourselves for jihad so that
we succeed and kill all infidels and the polytheist. The brothers coming united on

fronts in Kashmir, Chechnya, Palestine, Afghanistan and Iraq for jihad in name
of Allah.

The jorney to the training at the site in Pakistan will end and training site
will locate to others in gulf states. To receive an order contact me.

Khadija1417@hotmail.com

"Do Jihad against the disbelievers with your hands and tongues." for Allah
suffereth not the reward to be lost of those who do good. (At-Tauba.120)

Within an hour of my posting the call to jihad, Rashid responded,
inquiring:

forgive my informality, my time is limited. perhapse it would be best to set up a
seperate e-mail using western names, something we could write as they do, as
acquaintances, hiding in plain sight. Do you follow my meaning?

I am due to enter the war zone soon, perhapse 120 fajir's from now.
Unfortunatly due to my position I will be bearing the arms of the enemy, thus
putting not only my soul, but the souls of our brave brothers and sisters in peril.
thus my position may not be as advantageous as one may assume. it may be
best if I could arrange to meet in person with a contact once I am over there.
that being the case I would like to know how I may show that I am a friend and
willing to give my life for Allah's <swt> glorious will.

i must go.

i pray your fasts are not too hard this holy month.

salaam,

Abdul Rashid

His reply sent chills down my spine. He had taken the bait, and the
action was on.

I never rush to reply to my targets, because I vowed early on not to
forget that I am not a native Arabic speaker, and it takes time to pre-

pare an effective and believable response tailored to my target. Though I could tell Rashid was in the U.S.—and a native English speaker—I still took my time in crafting my follow-up to him. After all, if he was a U.S. citizen, his citizenship guaranteed him certain rights and protections, and in order to effectively vet his intentions without violating the law I would need to walk a fine line.

In planning my Rashid probe, I carefully analyzed exactly what Rashid was saying to me through his messages and how I would respond. I also set about gathering his Internet tracks and connecting all the dots to see who he was and what I could learn about him. I decided that I wanted to project the image of a midlevel al-Qaeda operative working as a recruiter. I felt this role would be effective because he had said that his position with the Army was his leverage going forward.

In the end, it took less than an hour to tie Rashid and the email address almujahadeen47@yahoo.com to one Ryan G. Anderson. I learned that Anderson was a Specialist with the Washington Army National Guard's 81st Brigade located out of Fort Lewis, Washington. Now I was really concerned. In looking at the activities and functions of the 81st Brigade, I learned that it was set to deploy to Iraq in February of 2004—only three months away.

Many conflicting thoughts flooded my mind about what Anderson's real intentions might be by alluding to a desire to defect to al-Qaeda and offer his life for Allah while an active member of the U.S. military. I told myself he must be naive and playing around. However, if he was in earnest, I had a serious problem on my hands. I approached every stage of my involvement with Anderson with caution and as much objectivity as I could muster.

Over the next couple of weeks, he wrote complaining about the liberal bastion of Seattle, and bragged about his superior grasp of politics, religion, history, and weapons. He alluded to an internal anguish and brewing conflict that had been raging inside him, as a convert to Islam, regarding America's conflict in Iraq, which he perceived as oppressing his fellow Muslims.

As my dossier on Anderson grew, his Internet footprints were invaluable. I found other email identities that tied into both his true identity as Spec. Ryan Anderson and his Muslim alter ego, Amir Abdul-Rashid.

On the Internet I found that he used several aliases such as: "Spec. R. G. Anderson," "Andy Ronson," "Al Mujahideen," "Al Muj," "Amir Abdul-Rashid," "Panzergrenadier," "F. J. Ikari," "ShinjiIkari," "Ryan 'Shinji' Anderson," and "Gunfighter84." By cross-tying Anderson's online identities with the email identities of almujahadeen47@yahoo.com, panzergrenadier@yahoo.com, Gunfighter84@hotmail.com, sovietskii_soyuz@hotmail.com, and ryan.anderson7@us.army.mil, I compiled appendix after appendix of each and every post he made on various sites.

I was also able to chart the process of his conversion to Islam by identifying and analyzing all his posts at sites that served converts to Islam. I learned of his guns and weapons interests by following all his messages at weapons forums, including how he built his own AK-47 rifle. On the weapons sites, he bragged about being a sniper in the Army, though he wasn't. He claimed the Army recognized his superior skills in weapons and warfare tactics and strategy, and had even secretly sought his counsel in these areas. In fact, Anderson was a tank commander for the M1-A1 and M1-A2 Abrams tanks. His flights of fancy and disengagement from reality disturbed me. The profile I was developing was of a genuinely misguided individual with something of a Jekyll and Hyde persona.

In 2003, Army Spec. Ryan Anderson was twenty-six years old. In complete counterpoint to how 9/11 had "radicalized" me, Anderson was an American military man whose 9/11 experience, oddly, had driven him to become a Muslim with dreams of terrorism. Throughout his life growing up in America, Anderson was always looking for a way to fit in but never quite did. During college, he became obsessed with warfare and military history, graduating with a BA in military history. However, after 9/11, Anderson became increasingly alienated from traditional America and found himself ever more drawn to radical Islam. In early 2002, he converted, with the intention of becoming a mujahideen to pursue jihad. At the same time, he joined the U.S. Army National Guard. He studied firearms, especially automatic weapons—his studies culminated with the homemade AK-47, the Kalashnikov, the true weapon of a mujahideen holy warrior.

I would later learn that Anderson had always thought of himself as deserving of and destined for greatness, but it had eluded him throughout his life. He blamed his failure to attain importance on all other elements of his life—never taking responsibility for his own part in his perceived failures.

During his later court-martial, it would be revealed that Anderson believed his family, friends, and Army tank crew were all conspiring against him to keep him from reaching the level of success and achievement that he believed he deserved. This would be his primary motivation for attempting to defect and join al-Qaeda, betraying his tank crew and his country.

Anderson's court-martial would provide a glimpse into the twisted world in which he existed. After joining the Army in 2002, he had tried to create an aura of intellectual superiority over his fellow soldiers. He even claimed credit for many of the military feats featured in the news. But his fellow soldiers weren't buying it, and frequently tormented him for boasting about his alleged "secret activities" with the Army brass. This further fed his resentment, and eventually led him to al-Qaeda. He felt he had finally found a group and ideology with which he identified and which would appreciate his self-proclaimed brilliance, talent, and flair for warfare. Anderson believed that al-Qaeda was the vehicle that would finally lead him to the destiny and fate he desired.

It was now November 7, 2003. I had been following Anderson since October 6 and had exchanged only a few messages with him so far. However, I had a pretty clear idea of what I was dealing with: an individual in the U.S. military claiming a deep desire to defect to al-Qaeda to embark down the path of jihad. Given that his unit was set to deploy to Iraq in a matter of months, I knew I had to find a way to route all my information to the military and allow them to decide what, if any, threat Anderson presented.

I knew his access to military information was what would excite a true al-Qaeda operative, so I started communicating with him along those lines. I told him one of my duties to al-Qaeda was to prove that he would be worthy to the brotherhood, so I needed to confirm the things he said before we took him in. He wrote, "How are you going to be able to do this?" He was very eager.

As soon as he knew I was interested, he took over, and I let him. This was critical to avoiding later allegations of entrapment. If he takes the lead, there's no entrapment there.

I knew one thing for sure—I wasn't going to submit this to the FBI tip line. After all, Anderson was a military subject, and I knew enough to know that they deal with their own.

I decided to contact the Department of Homeland Security to see if they could steer me in the right direction. I wanted a specific path, to ensure that the investigation didn't fall into any bureaucratic black hole at the Pentagon or Defense Department.

To my chagrin, however, DHS instructed me that the best place to start in trying to route my Rashid case was through my local FBI field office in Great Falls. I was not pleased, suspecting that DHS in fact didn't know what to tell me and was using the local FBI as a default. However, I followed the instructions given by DHS, and waited to be contacted by the Great Falls field office and advised on how I should proceed.

Later that morning, I got a call from FBI Special Agent James Wilson, asking if there was a time when they could come up to Conrad and discuss this "information" I had on a possible terrorist threat from a member of the military. I was not interested in having the FBI coming to my home and told Agent Wilson, "No, I would prefer to come to your office to discuss this matter." The rest of my conversation with Agent Wilson didn't go well. It was partly my fault. I was nervous. No one in the world, not even my husband Randy, knew I had spent hundreds of hours infiltrating terrorist websites and chat rooms posing as a Muslim holy warrior. I wasn't ready to share this secret. In my effort to maintain separation of my real life from the FBI or anything of an official nature, I was being evasive with personal details during my conversation with Agent James Wilson, which probably didn't inspire confidence. I told Agent Wilson that my purpose in making contact with the FBI was simply to pass along some vital information related to a member of the U.S. Army in the State of Washington who was trying to defect to al-Qaeda before his National Guard unit deployed to Iraq. I proceeded to inform Wilson that the information and materials I had that I wanted to pass along needed to fall into the hands of someone who might be able to prevent the deaths of American soldiers at the hands of this rogue member of the Army.

Agent Wilson sounded like he thought he was dealing with yet another wacko with fantasies of apprehending terrorists. I could tell he was annoyed to be stuck with me, and could imagine him shooting looks at his co-workers, making circles by the side of his head to indicate he was on the phone with a crazy person. Because I was a woman, I think, he threw a little extra sarcasm in his tone. There was no reason to make an immediate appointment, he said. "Why don't you just wait and drop this stuff off the next time you're in Great Falls?"

I could hear him smirking, but I wasn't going to let it get to me. This wasn't a pair of jeans I needed to return to J.C. Penny. I had come across something on the Internet that threatened our country. As a judge who had conducted many criminal trials, I recognized that the guy making the threat had the means and motive to carry it out. I said I wasn't going to wait.

"Can't you explain it to me on the phone?" said Wilson.

"It's too complicated," I said. "But I can tell you it involves a uniformed person and I think the information should be routed directly to the military."

"And how do you think I'm supposed to do that?"

Suddenly I was the one feeling impatient. The FBI was supposed to be part of an efficient, integrated, international effort to stop terrorism. But this agent didn't even know how to contact someone in the military. Worse, he was brushing off a citizen with real information about a serious threat. Again I pressed him for an appointment and again he resisted.

However, while sitting there in my office at home compiling all of the information and materials I had prepared on my Rashid case, I decided that I would rather keep a safe distance from officially meeting with the FBI and called Agent Wilson back to let him know that

I'd rather not meet in person but that I would send him copies of my stuff or answer his questions over the phone.

Since no one at home knew what I had been up to online, I wasn't ready to have the FBI call my house. I decided to use my trump card. "Listen," I said. "I can tell you that I'm a judge."

"A judge of what?" he answered, as if he expected the answer to be "pies."

"Of a court in Montana," I said, "and I'll show you my state identification when I get there."

The "judge card" didn't help as much as I had hoped it would. Wilson's voice still dripped with disdain. But he did agree to see me. Before leaving the house I made one last check of the materials I had put together, and reassured myself that the documents were clear, and so precisely indexed and highlighted that even a casual reader would be alarmed at their contents.

Sixty miles of interstate highway separate my home in Conrad, a quiet farm town in northern Montana, and the city of Great Falls to the south. Tourists taking in the Western scenery—big sky, rolling plains, grazing cattle—might need more than an hour to cover the distance. On that cold gray afternoon, I kept my foot on the accelerator pedal on my red Pontiac Grand Prix, speeding along at nearly eighty. Alone with my thoughts, I reviewed what I was going to say when I got to the regional field office of the Federal Bureau of Investigation.

My first contact with federal authorities was the year before, when I'd submitted the information to the tip line about the Jordanian who claimed to have Stinger missiles. It had gone well. I had this in mind when National Guard tank crewman Ryan Anderson (aka Amir Abdul-Rashid) came along with his pleas for help in defecting to al-Qaeda. Of course, the Great Falls, Montana, field office of the FBI is a long way from the task force protecting New York, but even with Agent Wilson's attitude, I still hoped this past experience would help me.

Having grown up at my father's side, and having worked with police in Conrad for years, I understood how certain kinds of men responded to assertive women. I knew when I was likely to get the dumb blonde treatment. I wasn't going to let them get away with it. When I got to the bank building where they kept their office, I made sure I had my state-issued credentials and carefully gathered up my materials. I felt confident as I entered the lobby and climbed up the stairs to the second floor.

A big decal with the FBI seal—"Fidelity, Integrity, Bravery"—was stuck to the glass door of the field office. I pressed the buzzer and identified myself on an intercom before they let me inside. As I opened the door, I saw four men, dressed in jeans and sport shirts with pistols on their hips, sitting casually at a rectangular conference table. They were so relaxed they could have been playing cards, or swapping stories about the one that got away. No one seemed especially impressed by my arrival. I could see one of the agents bite his cheek to keep from laughing as I introduced myself. Wilson, who was a stocky guy about five feet eight inches tall with thick glasses, finally identified himself, got out of his chair, and came over to talk.

"I don't want to take up a lot of your time," I said, "so let's just cut through the nonsense. I heard your skepticism on the phone, and I admit I might feel the same way if I was in your position. But I'm not a crackpot. I know what I'm doing. This guy is part of a tank crew in the Washington National Guard. He's shipping out in February and wants to defect. It's going to be up to you to make sure the right thing gets done."

With these words, Wilson's demeanor shifted. His face became serious and focused. He asked me how I came upon Anderson and looked through the report I had put together, which included the key emails. I tried to explain the jihadist website and how al-Qaeda and its supporters operated in cyberspace, but when I asked if we could go online to demonstrate, he explained that the FBI field office was still not connected to the Internet.

"If we need to use the Internet," he confessed, "we have to walk over to the library."

Fortunately, the paper printouts and the work I had done to identify Anderson persuaded him that I had discovered something important. When I asked about contacting someone in the Department of Defense—I assumed some channel of communication existed—Agent Wilson said he wasn't sure who to call.

"What about Malmstrom Air Force Base?" I asked. Six miles east of Great Falls, Malmstrom is mainly a missile base and, as we quickly learned, home to a single intelligence officer. As it turned out, he was very interested in what I had, and he asked me to stay until he could meet me.

For a moment I thought that with Wilson taking me seriously and the Defense Department on its way, the boys sitting around the field office might cut me some slack, but they didn't. I stood there alone while Wilson rejoined them and they carried on as if I wasn't there.

When the Air Force representative showed up, I didn't wait for Wilson to brief him. I took over, explaining that I had found this tank crew member set to deploy in February and ready to defect to al-Qaeda. Suddenly, the mood in the office shifted. Now I was having the important conversation, and the agents at the table were being left out.

"I'm not crazy," I said. "I have no mental illness. I'm just a judge up in Conrad who got very motivated after 9/11 and started studying the whole subject of terrorism. I took a big chance coming out of my safety zone to give you this stuff. Just take the information and look into it. I couldn't live with myself if it stopped with me. Now it's in your hands." With that, I shook their hands and thanked them for their time. As I left, they seemed very confused. But all I could feel was relief that I had done everything I could.

On the drive home I didn't even consider telling anyone, including Randy, how I had spent the day. The meeting had taken much longer than I expected, but I could still make it home in time to make dinner and get the kids started on homework. If he asked how my day was, I'd skirt the question, with something like, "Oh, it was good," which would be true. After all, I had managed to get a very reluctant federal bureaucracy to accept responsibility for Ryan Anderson. I felt happy and relieved.

The feeling wouldn't last. The next day, Agent Wilson called me at court. He had started to check the materials I had given him and realized he would need some time to do the job. I told him I wasn't in a private setting. He gave me his cell phone number, and I called him back later in the day, when I was alone. It was then that he asked, "Would you be able to keep him talking?" When I said I would, he asked if I knew what constituted entrapment. I reminded him that I was a judge.

When Wilson didn't press the issue, I felt we might be reaching a certain understanding. If the FBI needed me to continue dealing with Anderson for a little while longer, until they could take over, I would. Then I asked Wilson for an email address where he might receive copies of my communications with Anderson.

"Um, that could take a bit," he replied. "I have to see if I can get permission to open an email account somewhere."

Any hope that I might be rid of this case disappeared in that moment. If Agent Wilson wasn't able to receive email, and needed to go up the chain of command to remedy this problem, then he certainly wasn't prepared to take over my online work. I asked for his fax number, and agreed to send him printouts of my exchanges with Anderson. As we said good-bye, I accepted the fact that this duty—to track and prevent a would-be traitor from wreaking havoc on our military—would be mine for a while yet.

I had no way of knowing at the time, when I drove to Great Falls to meet with Agent Wilson for the first time, that this meeting would eventually bring my two worlds—my regular life as a judge, wife, and mother and my secret online realm filled with terrorists and danger—into head-on collision. An American soldier would be prosecuted for attempted espionage and imprisoned for life. My entire family would be imperiled, and the foundation of my very existence would be rocked. But I didn't know any of this.

One of the concerns that I had when Agent Wilson asked me if I would continue to keep Anderson talking while they "got their ducks in a row," was whether I would end up having to be a witness in any subsequent prosecution. I was concerned about the prospect of having to be a witness because I was a sitting judge at the time and worried about the appearance of any impropriety. Though I was satisfied that the Internet work I was doing didn't present any ethical dilemma, I simply didn't want to find myself in the middle of any high-profile court case at the same time I was a sitting judge. Agent Wilson assured me that my continued involvement with the Anderson case would end at a certain point where the case would be handed off from me to the FBI and then to the Army. At the point of handoff, the FBI would protect my identity in the case, and I was promised that I wouldn't have to testify. After all, I was a judge and had no intention of ever finding myself to the left of the bench. When they were ready to jump in, this case would be off my back and in the lap of the FBI and Army. In hindsight, I should have known better.

I had come to work closely with two members of the 7Seas group—the leader of the group whose screen name at itshappening .com was "Rogue," who resided in Idaho; and an individual who used the screen name "Hammy," out of Canada—over the preceding summer, and I decided to let them in on the case—one of my more unfortunate choices, I would later learn. One of the reasons I did it at the time was that I wasn't sure I could trust Agent Wilson or the FBI. Their chilly reception had left me dubious. I was concerned that if something went wrong—though I had no idea what that might actually be—I wanted others with knowledge of the case who could back me up down the road. But trusting Rogue would prove to be my biggest mistake. On the other hand, deciding to include Hammy in my revelation would prove to be the one aspect of this disclosure about the Anderson case that worked in my favor. I would come to trust Hammy very much, and to this day I hold him in the highest regard and trust him with my life, which is a big step in the trust chain for me.

WITH ANDERSON'S NATIONAL GUARD UNIT deployment date of February 2004 looming, time was of the essence. By now, it was the end of November 2003. After every communication with Anderson, I documented everything and updated the profile to avoid any wheel-spinning or counterproductivity. I faxed all my documentation to the Great Falls office, and they, in turn, faxed it to Salt Lake City. From there it would make its way to the Army authorities.

I quickly grew frustrated with this antiquated procedure, and with having to wait for any direction or insight. A few days in, I told Agent Wilson, "This isn't going to work if I wait around for you to tell me what to say. This guy is impatient . . . breathing down my neck for some action . . . and indicating that he is running out of time. If I am going to keep him in my loop and on the hook, I have to keep him interested and talking to me."

Meanwhile, Anderson's words were beginning to show signs of paranoia. Just before midnight on November 8, 2003, Anderson confided his fears to me: " . . . I am concerned, however slightly, that this might be a trap." "I do not believe anything beyond the peace I find in my prayers," he said and proceeded to suggest that we adopt Western names, stating that he would be "Andy," I would be "George," and we would communicate in code using casual English and new email accounts.

When I read his note, I had to smile. After weeks of posting from a web address that included the word "mujahideen" he had suddenly realized he might be attracting the attention of U.S. authorities. As Khadija, his wise Muslim brother, I wrote to agree to his strategy, and in language calculated to sound like a native Arab struggling with English, added, "Please let me know more what you want to do and how we can do our duties as Muslims."

With our new aliases, our alleged "cover" would be that we were old schoolmates from Washington State University, where Anderson graduated in 2002.

Though Anderson advised that I would now be known to him as "George," he did not specify what type of email account to open for our new round of communications. So in an effort to not deviate from my role as an al-Qaeda operative, I selected an Islamic email provider, dawah.znn.com, and opened my new account with the address george@dawah.znn.com. The last email I would send as Abu Khadija to Anderson would be to provide him with my new email address as George.

As I began my predawn prowl through the world of online jihad the next morning, my heart skipped a beat when I opened the inbox for George's email account and saw Anderson's new email address. Though the screen name was "Andy," the actual address appeared as "Ryan Anderson" sovietskii_soyuz@hotmail.com. At this point, I had given no indications to Anderson that I was in fact aware of his true identity, so I was quite surprised to see it right there in his new email. Quite an oversight on his part. In any case, I decided to make no mention of it.

Again, I let him take the lead, to further ward off any claims of entrapment down the road. My "long-lost college buddy" Andy wrote:

Hey George,

Just wanted to drop you a line and see what was new . . .I love guns, but cleaning them THAT MUCH??? (sigh) Oh well, I don't want to get caught with my pants down! Those terrorists can hit right when you don't expect them! I don't know if you've been following the news but it seems the fighters are coming in from other parts of the world. A real alliance of evil . . . (yes, I still like George Bush, even though he's sending us there, he's the guy I voted for, and I'll probably vote for him again.) Anyway, so what's up with you? I haven't talked to you since you graduated, man. I already forgot what you were going to do after graduation. . . . I remember you were majoring in . . . engineering? Is that right. It's been too long. Did you and that one girl ever get married . . . I just remember she was a nice girl . . . and she liked guns too—nothing sexier than a woman with a rifle . . . My wife is still kind of a kid . . . she still drinks (yech) and really has no faith . . . Well, I gotta run, going to enjoy my last nights of 'freedom.' . . . hey man, take care and write me soon . . .

Andy

I, as George, replied:

Andy,

It is so good to hear from you . . . From the tone of your email I can tell you are still same old Andy! Ever one for adventure! Your memory serves you well. I did go into engineering. I am working in electronics and find it very satisfying. But I have been pursuing physics graduate degree on part-time basis, when money is available. No I haven't taken marriage vows as of yet. It is hard to find a nice wholesome woman these days that is true to her faith and willing to submit to her husband . . .

George

As our communications progressed into November, I found myself struggling to balance the Anderson case with the trappings of my normal life—specifically, the coming holiday rush. One of the things I love most about the holidays is cooking the Thanksgiving and Christmas meals. Of course, I shop for presents and decorate, but mostly because Christmas, for me, is all about kids and providing them with some magic, surprise, and excitement at the end of each year. Though it is nice to receive presents, I enjoy giving them much more. Since I became a mother, watching my kids wake up to see what Santa has brought them each year and giving them the gifts they have carefully put on their Christmas wish lists each year is one of my brightest moments.

That holiday season, I was careful to give no hint to anyone of all that had been actually occupying my thoughts that year. I was only too happy to keep this area of my life in a tightly wrapped box. In fact, late one night, while wrapping gifts to set under the tree, I thought, "If only I could wrap up this Anderson case and put it in a pretty box to be delivered with a label that read 'To: The FBI, From: Shannen Rossmiller . . .' what a gift that would be to give."

One thing that was clear from our email exchanges was that Anderson wanted to have this all done before Christmas. He wanted details for the defection process, and he was becoming more and more impatient, asking whether he and I would ever meet in person.

A few days before Christmas 2003, in one email exchange evidencing his adamancy, Anderson wrote:

> AK, Let's do this, I have to be back on base Monday night, so we have between now and then. I provided you with a cell number last time. Have my contact call me on it, as I will be off base . . . just make sure the brother is careful with what he says. I would prefer to meet at a Masjid or a restaurant for a meal as it would provide a good setting. Perhaps Seattle Center if the contact is willing. My time draws to a close in these United States, so let's make the most of what we've got.
>
> Salaam AR

It was becoming nearly impossible to appease Anderson while awaiting word from the FBI on a date for the handoff. I advised the FBI that I was going to wait until Christmas day to send him a reply and would use the date the crusaders celebrate their infidel holiday as a twist to keep Anderson hanging on. I would promise him that the details he so desperately craved would be coming in the next few days.

After the kids had finished opening their Christmas gifts and were happily busying themselves with their haul, and Randy was out in his shop tending to his new RC airplane kits and accessories, I checked the progress of my Christmas bird in the oven and went back into the office to send my friend Anderson a nice gift for the holiday. I had been writing and rewriting different versions of the email for the past two days, only settling on the wording I wanted earlier that morning. I sat down at the computer and reread my reply, double-checking all the points I wanted to make and how they should be stated. I titled it "your details," and as I hit the send button, I said out loud, "Merry Christmas, traitor." I'm sure I was smiling from ear to ear. The email was simple and straightforward. I imagined Anderson's excitement upon reading it:

AR,

It is so good to hear from you and to sense the enthusiasm you embrace our struggle. It is fitting that we should exchange these communications on the day of the Crusader celebrations. Isa is a great prophet but to call him God blasphemes.

The brothers understand the urgency and the time constraints that you are operating under.

He is a dedicated soldier and I believe that the two of you will have many things in common. He is very eager to meet you and assist you to move further along the path to serve as a soldier of Allah. He and the rest of the brothers are striving to tidy up our current assignments so that we can more fully focus upon the promise that you hold for our work in Allah's name.

The brothers understand your concern for security and that is part of our standard procedure. Your contact has been made aware of your cell phone number and direct contact will be made as soon as is practical. My brother, please give us as much of your schedule that is foreseeable. Your contact must complete his task but discussing arrangements is his next work.

The way of a soldier is one of patience my brother. Submission to the will of Allah allays all fears and sweeps away all doubts.

Peace be with you,

Assalamu Alalikum Wa Rahmatullah

AK

That day, I really felt that I understood the importance of giving to others before receiving anything for oneself at that moment. I felt at peace and happy knowing that I had done a good deed. If I could prevent Anderson from harming any soldiers, or ever setting foot in Iraq, then all my efforts were worth it. That was something I could live with.

My conversations with Anderson taught me a lot about a certain type of terrorist profile. He was a braggart and chatterbox, eager to hand over sensitive and confidential information and materials without my even having to ask. He was also a person who sought great importance in this world, and had been denied it in most facets of life. He was bent on proving his worth to al-Qaeda. It was a pattern that would repeat itself many times.

Over the months as Rashid and Abu Khadija, Andy and George, AR and AK, Anderson willingly provided information on current and projected troop locations and military activities in Iraq, schematics and plans for the M1-A1 and M1-A2 Abrams tanks, and other important information that would almost certainly result in the death of U.S. soldiers. I became less and less concerned for Anderson's fate, as he was proving at each stage that he was aware of his actions and the consequences that could result. He required no prodding or encouragement. He had been in the driver's seat the whole time. Any suspicion I may have had early on that Anderson was a misguided or unstable individual was gone. In my legal and personal judgment, he was a true enemy of my country. I had resolved that he was deserving of whatever cold hard fate lay in front of him.

The day after Christmas, I got the chilling reply to "your details." I could tell he was trying to downplay his excitement, but I had offered up enough to him to convince him it was all coming together. He wrote:

AK,

It is my dream that we remember and celebrate all the great prophets of Allah (swt) with such joy and reverance as our cousins claim to give to prophet Isa, and it is much agreed that their worship of a flesh and blood man is a blaspheme to be sure—one of the reasons I left their corrupted ranks and sought God's true path in Islam. I would enjoy some time discussing the historical issues here with you, it is a most fascinating study in human psychology.

To be sure this Crusader holiday is a badly perverted one, they now do not even make an attempt to bring God into it anymore, but use it in worship of material wealth and secular society, the only deity their children pray to on this 'holy-day' is the one called Santa Claus, an image cobbled togather of tribal pagan gods of the winter solstice, and of ancient Roman deities which they supposedly reviled . . . such is the way of the non-believer.

Anyway, to the matter at hand- my schedule until Monday is simple, I will be with family and friends and with my wife. She is working every day except this one though (she works in a small retail outlet for some cousins of hers in Seattle) so I will have freedom of movement during the days. I intended to go shooting in the mountains as well during the morning on Sunday but that is not a vital activity. After that I will return to the Army and will be training for the foreseeable future—perhaps at the end of the next month we will be leaving the state—I wish I could give you some sort of certainty about where we are going and what we are doing but the truth of the matter is they change it on us as the warmongers at the Pentagon and in the government see fit, one morning we will be told we are to guard a depot in Qatar by mid March, the next evening we are told we will be in the so-called "Green-zone" in Baghdad in the end of February—it is both disturbing and demoralizing to the troops, but as any good soldier, they do as they are told and live with the changes as a fact of life.

Every day more the cheap morals of these people sickens and saddens me, they are not bad people, but the culture they are in has their manners foul and their humor course, they seek nothing more than carnal pleasures, financial gain, and pleasure in alcohol and other like escapes for themselves. Their marrages are sadly 'open' and adultury on the parts of husbands seems to be a celebrated practice with pornography being seen in the open daily and perverted, demeaning sexual humor the talk of the hour . . . . every hour. I long only for the companionship of good Muslims and the love of my wife, and, inshallah, of children in the years to come.

Lastly, as a word of caution. . . . it is not that I do not trust in your veracity, or your identity, but should this situation turn out to be a trick from those who would seek to decieve a honest brother, or should this be used by forces who gather against us, I will not be unprepared to defend myself when we make contact, nor will I hesitate to force our enemies to martyr me should they attempt to capture myself and any other brother found with me. A soldier resists surrender with his last breath and greets passage into the open arms of Allah with joy and eagerness.

Asalaam Alaaykum,

AR

I had always expected he would eventually threaten the use of violence or weapons, but this email raised the stakes. Here was a guy who not only wanted his fellow soldiers killed but was willing to martyr himself if anything went wrong. This was a whole new landscape.

I didn't reply immediately, mostly because I had no new information or details to relay to him. The next morning, as I settled in to start my day trolling the jihadist sites, I checked my Khadija email inbox, and there was a message waiting for me from Anderson titled "making contact." It said:

Running out of time here AK, would be good if I could have an idea on when this is all going down.

Salaam

AR

Again, I didn't reply. I had nothing new to tell him and I was growing impatient myself waiting for the FBI. I knew they had to find the right people to coordinate an undercover meeting, but I feared I would lose him if it took much longer.

The next day, December 28, my fears were confirmed. I opened his latest email to find that he was attempting to say "farewell" and let me know that if I failed to hook him up with one of the "brothers" soon, he would wait until he arrived in Kuwait with his brigade. I was truly panicked at the thought of him as a loose cannon in Iraq, working with his crew while simultaneously seeking out al-Qaeda contacts on his own. Considering the constant and unstructured flow of mujahideen coming into Iraq to fight the Americans, it wouldn't be hard.

With the FBI still working toward the point of handing the case off from me to them, I decided it was paramount to keep Anderson talking. I sent him a reply later that night telling him that my group of brothers worked in intelligence for the mujahideen outside of the United States, supporting jihad operations. I told him that his contact was from an operational arm of my group located in the United States and would be contacting him soon, but until then he was to continue to advise me of his status.

This worked better than expected, as he took the opportunity to open up even further with me. He told me how impressed he was to finally know about "my group" and how he felt every day as though he was "sitting on the wrong side of the mirror." He also said he had been trying to find his way into "this sort of thing" for a while, and that his heart felt at peace and his fear abated as he "pursued this path you are aiding me on."

On January 3, 2004, the FBI finally told me they were in a position for me to hand off the case, and that my role as midlevel al-Qaeda operative Abu Khadija to Anderson was finally over. I felt such relief and pride knowing that this traitorous American soldier would not get the opportunity to harm his fellow soldiers or anyone else.

I would later learn that Seattle's FBI Division worked in conjunction with two undercover Defense Intelligence Agency (DIA) agents out of Fort Hood, Texas, to set up the in-person meeting with Anderson. One of the DIA agents, who was to be his al-Qaeda contact, went by the name of "Omar" and appeared Middle Eastern, wearing traditional Islamic clothing, while the other agent posed as his liaison here in the U.S., dressed in typical Western garb.

The meetings took place over two days, the first in the back of a nondescript van in a parking garage next to the Seattle Space Needle, recorded by a hidden camera. On the video, Anderson discusses the same intentions he expressed to me regarding his defection from the Army to al-Qaeda and the reasons for his choice.

The second meeting took place at a Barnes & Noble in Seattle, where Anderson handed over scanned copies of his military ID, passport, and driver's license, as well as documents containing more information and specs related to the M1-A1 and M1-A2 Abrams tanks, and updated information for troop locations in Iraq and the Balad Air Base. Anyone could see he was hopelessly out of his league at this point.

Though I was relieved that the meetings had gone down without incident or violence, by the end of January, he had still not been arrested. I was growing concerned that something was wrong and that he would be allowed to deploy with his brigade. Something inside me didn't fully trust what I was being told by the FBI. So I began searching the Seattle news outlets on a fairly regular basis, looking for word of an arrest, or anything about the upcoming deployment of Anderson's brigade.

Finally, on February 7, in the Seattle *Post-Intelligencer,* there was an article about the deployment ceremony held at the Tacoma Dome for Anderson's 81st Armor Brigade. To my shock, Spec. Ryan Anderson was quoted about his upcoming deployment to Iraq. Of the roughly three thousand soldiers in Anderson's brigade, I thought, what was the likelihood Anderson himself would be singled out and interviewed?

Knowing that the undercover meetings had occurred two weeks earlier, were the Army and the FBI taking the threat seriously, or had they decided to drop the case? The window of time before Anderson's deployment was now down to nine days. Nothing about this situation or case felt right at that moment. I felt sick thinking all my efforts could have been for nothing. My questions would go unanswered for another five days.

On February 12, I took a day off from work because I had scheduled a dentist appointment for my youngest daughter. Around 11:00 that morning, I received a telephone call from Agent Wilson asking me to come down to his office in Great Falls that afternoon. I was not feeling particularly cooperative at this point, since no one had returned any of my phone calls for the past five days. I told Agent Wilson I wasn't sure that I could make it with such short notice, and that I would need to find someone to take my daughter to the dentist. Agent Wilson simply told me that it was in my interest to come to his office that afternoon and that he could not discuss anything further over the phone.

By now, I felt like a worthless pawn at the hands of the FBI. I was able to arrange for a friend to take my daughter to the dentist that afternoon and left for Great Falls after lunch, arriving at the FBI office around 1:30. Wilson took me into their small conference room and shut the door. He advised me that Anderson would be arrested out in Washington some time that afternoon. A few minutes later, we received word from the FBI out in Seattle that the arrest was accomplished without incident. I was told that the FBI was in the process of transferring Anderson from their custody to the CID Division of the Army and would be detained in the jail at Fort Lewis until he appeared before the military court. I didn't know what to think, except that it didn't feel real.

Agent Wilson also said that news of the arrest would be breaking anytime, and that by midafternoon it would be a nationwide story. He asked me to not contact the media and inform them of my involvement in the case—which I had no intention of doing. I was pleasantly surprised when he went on to thank me for pushing the importance of the case from the beginning, and not missing red flags.

I left Agent Wilson's office that afternoon feeling satisfied. My mind was racing on the drive home, full of unanswered questions. The one thought that I remember clearly was being relieved that I had been able to complete my involvement in the Anderson case without Randy and my family finding out, and that they would never know of my involvement unless I decided to tell them. At the time, I truly believed the Anderson case was behind me, and that was the best place to leave it.

But I couldn't shelve my curiosity when it came to the news of Anderson's arrest. By the time I got home that afternoon, it was being reported on Fox News, CNN, and MSNBC. I flipped around the channels, trying to glean any new details while hurrying to get dinner started before Randy got home.

I figured my interest in the news that day wouldn't seem unusual, since the Anderson case would be right up my alley even if I hadn't been involved. But I hadn't anticipated how I would feel when I saw a picture of Anderson—that anonymous person in front of a computer screen two states away. I hadn't given much thought to what Anderson actually looked like, since he had always been a part of my virtual world. Until today, the only pictures I had seen of him were in the clothing of a mujahideen, holding the AK-47 rifle he had put together himself. His face was always covered with the red and white checkered *kaffiyeh* (head scarf)—with his eyes peering out as the only evidence of a face underneath. This was his Muslim identity—Amir Abdul-Rashid—pictures of the mujahideen fighter he dreamed he would one day be. Now, I was staring at Specialist Ryan Anderson—a young white male with a baby face. An innocent face.

The contrast of the picture with the enemy underneath disturbed me greatly. Still, as I went to sleep that night, I really believed that my life was going to return to normal. I was happy to think I would have had more free time on my hands. I had plenty to keep me busy: my efforts to pursue the jihadists at GIMG were always on the front burner, as well as the daily monitoring of the jihadist sites and the information flow relating to Iraq and Afghanistan.

The next day, I would meet the FBI agent who would become my saving grace, Special Agent Mark Seyler, who was out of the Helena Field Office. He informed me that he was the JTTF (Joint Terrorism Task Force) agent with the FBI in Montana, and that some discrepancies in the Anderson case had arisen that needed to be sorted out. This is when I discovered that Rogue, the leader of the 7Seas group, was now claiming that it was he, and not I, who had cracked the case, and that I would have to prove my involvement by authenticating the email evidence.

I would also learn that Rogue had a less than savory background, and had been making a living as an undercover drug informant for the FBI in Idaho. Clearly, when I told him about Anderson, Rogue could see that it was going to be a high-profile case, and before Anderson was arrested he had spoken to other members of the 7Seas group about claiming a large reward for the case. He would go on to claim that he had performed the email communications with Anderson and provided me with the information to send on to the FBI. Thank God each and every email I exchanged with Anderson contained my IP address in the email headers, allowing me not only to prove my involvement but also to secure the authenticity of the email evidence for Anderson's prosecution.

Special Agent Seyler, however, was a gift in disguise. As fate would have it, he was a fellow Montanan, my age, and we grew up in similar small towns and had similar backgrounds. I was thrilled to find someone I could relate to, who had no agenda and didn't set off my "danger" radar. For the first time since the FBI had entered my life, I relaxed. Agent Seyler and I became as close as we could in our delicate and uncharted circumstances.

It would be Mark whom the FBI would call on to sort out Rogue's claim to have been the operator in the Anderson case. Of course, he would also be the one to inform me that my involvement in it was far from over.

CHAPTER SIX

OPERATION
WHIRLPOOL

In 2003, another interesting individual popped onto my radar, through an online undercover operation I had developed with my colleague in Canada. I did not initially understand his significance to the upper echelon of al-Qaeda.

All of my online operations up until that time had relied upon my skill and chutzpah. Yet at the time, I felt an overwhelming need to kick things up a notch. I was ready to take my hunting further, to try to obtain more valuable and targeted information. Until then, I had focused primarily on getting my targets to up their ante. These operations were inherently limited in scope and value, because they depended on what the target chose to reveal.

We spent weeks planning and coordinating our targets and objectives for this new and risky operation. We decided to call it "Whirlpool," because we planned to attract and suck in radical and extremist targets. I wanted to target those individuals in the forums who appeared to be "in the know"—that is, members who discussed information that I had already verified. Sometimes these confirmations came through news reports, usually in the Arab and Middle East media. I wasn't interested in individuals who engaged in propaganda or simply voiced support for the jihadist and mujahideen cause. I wanted people with valuable information and connections, who harbored a definite intent to harm and target Western interests.

In any undercover operation, whether conducted in the real or virtual world, planning and preparation—selecting the best targets and the right bait to dangle in front of the jihadists—are critical. So we treated Operation Whirlpool, our new baby, with utmost care.

To the best of my knowledge, despite various attempts at remote viewing and psychological warfare, no one had yet achieved deep insight into a target's actual thoughts and behavioral processes on the Internet—not even the elements of the U.S. government that I was familiar with. This would require much more than simple analysis of the dynamics of the jihadist forums. If I was going to get in deeper to understand the makeup and mechanics of the individuals of interest to me, I would have to get closer. I needed to know what they coveted and valued, and why. I decided that the next best step for target infiltration would be to find a legal and viable way to get into their computers.

I wanted to know what my marks were really like offline. I needed to see the contrast between that and the profiles I had developed of them. I reasoned that if I could covertly infiltrate their lives through their computers, I could go deeper into their world of murder and mayhem online. However, it would require Trojan-type modules to gain backdoor access into a computer. I would have to determine the legality of this type of operation before initiating it. I knew that if I targeted any individuals in the U.S. or who used any U.S. Internet service providers, my actions could be construed as illegal as this presented a legal gray area.

The first step would be to establish the true location of targets, and whether any such targets appeared to be using proxy programs to mask their IP addresses. If so, I would not pursue them and risk the chance that they might be somewhere in the U.S. Operation Whirlpool would only pursue and target individuals outside of the U.S.

Operation Whirlpool brought together my skills at probing the behavioral components of a jihadist's mind and behavior with those of my colleague in Canada, a software developer who is also a nuclear physicist. Radical Islamists love images depicting the destruction of America and the West, and they had come to love and covet the documents and materials that allowed them to self-train themselves and others for jihad to become true mujahideen fighters. My colleague in Toronto and I decided that the best way to execute the Whirlpool bait would be to imbed an executable module into one of the manuals of the *Jihad Encyclopedia*. We chose the *Explosives Manual*. I decided that I would post as Abu Khadija in the forums, indicating that the *Explosives Manual* had been updated, which would prompt those members interested in explosives training information and materials to click and open my module.

These executable modules were the payload of Whirlpool, with content expressly designed to whet the appetite of my most desired targets. The trick was to make them so appealing and new that no terrorist worth his salt could possibly pass them up. I set to work accumulating images and documents from around the jihadist corners of the Internet, and found plenty of materials that made my online targets virtually salivate in anticipation.

I selected Abu Khadija for this mission because the real Abu Khadija was a known contributor to the *Jihad Encyclopedia,* giving it the appearance of credibility. I carefully selected three of the most popular and radical forums, and profiled the activity of the forum members who would be the best targets for the operation for a period of three weeks.

Back in 2003, any member of these forums could upload files into a thread for other members to click, open, view, or read. As such, it was easy to slip in zipped-up executable modules that would allow backdoor entry into my targets' computers.

The Whirlpool trap consisted of a simple piece of software designed by my Canadian partner to monitor Internet and computer usage. The bait and payload module were melded together in a simple yet elegant program written by my colleague in Canada. The Whirlpool bait, documents, and images were packaged together in a self-extracting zip file, intended to be deployed on the selected jihadist sites known to be habituated by violent and radical members, but not against any individual in particular. Whirlpool would be a throw-it-out-and-see-what-sticks kind of operation. We worked to combine the bait with our monitoring program and the payload module into yet another file—designed to give the appearance of a simple, self-extracting zip file.

In fact, it was an executable module whose function it was to unzip the bait, giving the viewer what he or she expected, while simultaneously covertly installing the monitoring software and then cleaning up all the unnecessary files from a target's computer. The target would think that he had simply unzipped a file containing the goodies that he sought, and from then on, the monitoring program would run quietly in the background, recording every keystroke, email address, and password entered on that computer. This information would then be uploaded to a separate and private web space designed to host all the information and materials we obtained from the Whirlpool net.

To our surprise, it worked. Potential targets began to open the bait module, and the monitoring program began to run as intended, yielding a glut of information from inside computers on the other side of the world. Much of it was meaningless, some of it funny; in these cases, we purged the information from the program. In fact, Whirlpool initially garnered *too many* targets and had to be whittled down in order for us to keep up. As more individuals were deactivated, we selected a handful that we believed were worth our time and effort and decided to focus on them and then removed the module from the forums.

As a member of the forums you could edit your posts and information posted up to a certain period of time, or until the thread was locked. In the latter case, if you wanted your post removed, you would have to contact the forum administrator. The initial Whirlpool module had been live in the three forums we had chosen for just under two weeks, so I was able to remove the posts without difficulty.

I was stunned by the magnitude of what the Whirlpool module revealed.

One of the individuals who took the Whirlpool bait was an individual I will call "Samir." I learned that Samir was operating under an undercover email ID in one of the jihadist forums selected for the operation. I had obtained and analyzed all of his Internet tracks and associated email addresses before confirming what I believed to be his identity—he then became one of the primary targets of Whirlpool, and all of his online activities were monitored several times daily and would be for almost a year.

Samir is a Sunni Muslim of Palestinian descent, a respected television journalist and reporter for various media outlets in the Arab world. He spent many years with the well-known Arab television network Al Jazeera but left the network in 2000 to become the bureau chief for Abu Dhabi TV, in Islamabad, Pakistan. I would learn that Samir was one of the few journalists who has met and interviewed Osama bin Laden. In 1998, Samir was contacted by representatives of al-Qaeda to come to Jalalabad, Afghanistan, and taken to an undisclosed location for the interview.

I also learned that Samir was the only journalist contacted directly by representatives of al-Qaeda on September 12, 2001, the day after the 9/11 attacks. A spokesman for the organization called his cell phone to advise him that bin Laden and al-Qaeda praised the attacks bestowed on America but disavowed any involvement or responsibility in them. It was well known that Samir had developed a rapport with bin Laden and al-Qaeda and sympathized with their radical Islamist ideology.

Once we realized Samir's value, he essentially became the entire Whirlpool operation, owing to the volume of communications his module produced that required translation and analysis on a daily basis. Since I was operating on a shoestring, with only my trusted Canadian colleague, we decided to allocate all the resources we had to Samir. After all, he might be as close to bin Laden as we would ever get. I dreamed that one day he would lead me directly to bin Laden. I reasoned that if al-Qaeda had Samir's cell phone number as recently as two years prior, he probably had viable and current contact with the man behind 9/11 and his terrorist group. He was the golden goose, and I was going to pursue him as carefully and diligently as possible.

Early each morning and late into the night, I translated the instant messages, emails, and documents sent and received through his email accounts. I copied all of the contacts in his email accounts and tried to connect the dots to any other information I had. I was not concerned with his journalistic contacts as with any I could relate to elements of al-Qaeda and the Taliban.

I carefully chronicled everything that came and went from his various email accounts, as well as the pattern he used to change his passwords to these accounts. I was breathless with excitement to be living inside the computer of one of the few people in the world who had met bin Laden, interviewed him. This was as close to any of the many tentacles of al-Qaeda as I ever expected to get.

Over the months that I monitored Samir, I intercepted several important nuggets of information and turned them over to the FBI. I also took the opportunity to befriend Samir in the jihadist forums as a purported fellow mujahideen supporter, never acknowledging that I was aware of his true identity. In time, he came to trust me, which was one of my primary goals.

From Samir's computer communications, I was able to construct a very good snapshot of his life, both personally and professionally. As bureau chief in Islamabad, he traveled, sometimes twice a month, from Islamabad to Kabul and talked of one day starting his own media company. He was a father and husband and talked of his Palestinian heritage and support for the reestablishment of a Palestinian state.

After a while, I concluded that Samir may be using these trips from Islamabad to Kabul to ferry the audio- and videotapes made by al-Qaeda that were eventually aired on the Arab television networks. I figured if he was moving al-Qaeda's tapes, it was also likely that they trusted him enough to get other information and materials to other intended recipients. Many months later, I would discover just how true this was.

One day in late October 2003, Samir was chatting via instant message with a person named "Walid" who had passed him what appeared to be geographical coordinates for some important location that was to be a "new base." I immediately took the coordinates and went looking for the location they represented.

I determined that the coordinates Walid had passed to Samir were for a location near a mountain area known as Tirich Mir, which is the highest mountain in the Hindu Kush region at 25,289 feet, near the border of Afghanistan and the lawless tribal areas of northwestern Pakistan. The town of Chitral, Pakistan, sits at the base of Tirich Mir in the Kunar Valley, part of Pakistan's lawless Federally Administered Tribal Areas. It was my belief at the time that Osama bin Laden was hiding in the Kunar Valley, where he enjoyed the protection of the local Pashtuns. I was determined to get a satellite image of the area to see what might be revealed about the establishment of this "new base."

In early November, I found a satellite imaging company called Digital Globe, where I could purchase high-quality satellite images of geographical coordinates around the world. When I received the satellite imagery of the area of the so-called new base, the picture showed a relatively flat area of land. In fact, it appeared as though the area had been groomed for a possible landing strip, perhaps to facilitate the transport in and out of the materials and supplies that would be needed for the establishment of this new base. My mind was racing. Could this be the key to locating bin Laden and bringing him to justice?

As Operation Whirlpool continued, I decided I would no longer interact with Samir in the jihadist forums. I felt it would be too easy to make a mistake. I reasoned that my direct dealings with him were not nearly as valuable as the information harvested from his computer each day.

In order to monitor the satellite imagery of the new base, I was incurring costs for each new image. Because I didn't want to alert Randy to the depth of my important work, I decided it would be smarter—and more affordable—to get a new image only every week or ten days.

I also figured that if the new base was being built quietly and under the radar, it would be a slow process. If I had learned one thing about the Arab and Middle East culture, it was that they are an infinitely patient people, quite the opposite of those living in our hurried Western culture. We want the results as soon as possible and don't consider the drawbacks, which doesn't always serve us well.

The simple landing strip I had seen in the first photo gradually grew longer and wider, then stopped. There was very little activity for a while, and I began to wonder if that was all there would be. Then, the first week of December, while translating the day's harvest, I saw an instant message chat between Samir and a man named Marwan, whose name I recognized from earlier communications. Marwan was telling Samir that the route from the base to Ayun (a village close to Chitral, Pakistan), to the brothers placed there, was where the new units would travel through. The message, though I couldn't understand it, obviously meant something to Samir, but I didn't see anything else from Marwan. This message included the first reference I had seen to a base since that of the October instant message from "Walid." It also contained the names of villages close to Chitral, which was the closest town to the coordinates I had been monitoring. Connecting the dots, I could only conclude that the purpose of the landing strip was to covertly fly people into the area for some unknown purpose, using small aircraft that could pass under conventional radar.

Meanwhile, I continued to research the Ayun village area near Chitral to determine what these new units might be and what importance they held. I would finally learn the answer in early January.

On January 4, 2004, Samir received an email from an individual named Ali Ahmad who referred to himself as the Mujahid from Yemen, claiming that he got Samir's contact info from a mutual friend.

The Mujahid from Yemen was requesting Samir's help in traveling to Pakistan to train with the mujahideen. He suggested that Samir sponsor his travel to Pakistan under the guise of a tourist.

The big picture was starting to emerge. The Mujahid addressed Samir as someone with the right connections, means, and resources to get him to the place where the mujahideen were training. Samir's response was to scold the Mujahid for contacting him in writing and said that they would only discuss the matter by satellite phone. I wished desperately for the number to Samir's satellite phone, but I hadn't come across any such thing in the many months I had been shadowing him.

Then, on January 12, I got my biggest break since Operation Whirlpool had begun.

The day before, Samir received an email from Marwan with a document attached. The body of the email simply instructed him that this important document was to be delivered to the Sheik Gilani in Lahore. I opened the document, dated January 14, 2004, which was four pages long and all in Arabic; it would take time to translate. I was able to make out the title, which was "The Special Clarification."

Whenever I sit down to translate large files, I first run them through the Arabic-English-Arabic software program I bought, to give me some idea of their importance or lack thereof. After reading the software-provided translation of the special clarification, I knew that clarifying the context would be critical to determining how valuable and important this find actually was. Thankfully, it had arrived on a Friday and I would have the weekend to work through it. As I took it apart sentence by sentence, it all seemed to relate to the new base–landing strip and the movement of people to Ayun. The first lines revealed the special clarification's creator and subject:

From the Islamic emirate in Afghanistan

Concerning the liberation of ninety-one departments in twenty region from

Afghanistan regions

It went on to describe the recent stationing of ninety-one units of Taliban and al-Qaeda fighters in twenty areas along the border of the Islamic Emirate of Afghanistan. I certainly felt that the special clarification was dated recently enough and had enough specific details to possibly provide the military some critical and actionable intelligence. Once I was sure of the translation, I packaged it up and sent it off to Mark, hoping that he would route it quickly enough for the right military folks to determine whether it was in fact actionable.

Later, I was reassured that the information was as "good as gold."

CHAPTER SEVEN

ARTICLE 32

I had managed, sometimes barely, to keep my life as a cyber spy secret from all of my family and friends. I did not want them to judge my actions or to tell me I was wasting my time. I reasoned that they would not understand the extent of what I had gotten myself into, and figured what they didn't know wouldn't hurt them.

Of course, this would all change.

It all went down during the Specialist Ryan Anderson case. They say that you can't go back and change the way things are, and knowing that, I eventually concluded I had to make the best of a bad situation.

Randy doesn't watch the news, and since we had decided after the computer crash of the previous year that all my work on the Internet was going to be "my thing," I didn't tell him about my involvement or Anderson's arrest. I was trying to keep things regarding my Internet work separate and apart from my carefully protected real life—the important thing was that the FBI would stop calling and coming to my house. I hoped things would go back to normal. Agent Seyler, whom I trusted more than anyone else in the FBI, didn't discourage this idea when he called the next morning. But he did ask if I would meet him in person to discuss how I might continue to help with Anderson's prosecution.

When I talked to Mark, he said the Army wanted me to testify, adding, "Would you be a cooperative witness or a hostile one?"

"Do you think I can do it in a closed-court setting?" I asked, because I was worried about terrorists learning my identity as well as there being any public knowledge of the work I had been doing following terrorist threats.

"I think you can."

"Then I'll do it."

MY TIME WAS RUNNING OUT. I only had two months (from February 12, when Anderson was arrested, until the end of March) before the Article 32 hearing was set to begin in May, and I had yet to tell Randy about the case. I waited until the very last minute, knowing that explaining this development to Randy would prove to be a slippery slope. I decided that at this point full disclosure was going to be the only way and so I outlined how to tell Randy about the case and what would likely transpire with me having to be a witness in a terrorism-related case. There was really only one way to do this and I was feeling anxious about his possible reaction considering the fact that he would now learn that his wife was doing much more on the Internet than simply following an interest in the subject matter of al-Qaeda and terrorism.

That evening Randy went out to the airfield where his club flies remote-control airplanes. As I drove up to the airfield, he noticed my car and looked surprised to see me. I got out of the car with the little cooler of beer I had brought with me. After he landed his plane, he asked me what I was doing out there. I told him that I wanted to see him flying and thought we could drink a few beers and talk. After consuming the beer I had brought with me, I started to tell him what I had come there to tell him. I started by saying that there was something important I had to tell him and wasn't sure how to. There really wasn't any way to segue into what was coming.

I could tell that he thought that I had come out to tell him about something that happened with our middle daughter because at the time she was our little lightning rod. I was stammering trying to get out what I needed to tell him and said, "I don't even know how to tell you this."

He said, "Well, is it important?" I replied, "Yes. It's kind of important." Randy's big brown eyes were getting even bigger.

In my mind, I thought I had outlined what I would tell him but had not figured out the boundaries of what I was going to say. I tried to downplay it and said I had been interested in al-Qaeda—he had known about this for a while now. "You know it was always my intention with my fascination and interest in the terrorist threats in the War on the Internet that it would stay in that context. I didn't think it would cross over into our lives—but it has."

"What are you talking about?" he asked.

I tried to explain that sometimes I like to chat and communicate with interesting people in these terrorist Internet sites. I went on to explain that what happened was that a couple of months ago I ran into this individual who showed up in one of these sites I had joined. But, he was posting in English instead of Arabic so he stood out to me and I started talking to him. Randy was trying to follow this. As I started to explain more of the story, I told him that the case involved a guy in the Army out in Washington whose National Guard unit was going to deploy to Iraq back in February but he had come into one of the Arab terrorist sites that I liked to follow and was looking to make contact with al-Qaeda to defect to their group once he arrived in Iraq. I also told him that the guy also tried to provide me information on the Army's Abrams tanks and other sensitive materials. Randy said, "Wait a minute. Why would he tell you this? What the hell are you talking about?" At this point I figured it was best just to lay it all out. He said, "What are you trying to tell me?"

I proceeded to tell him about Anderson and what he had attempted to do to highlight the importance of the case—and probably to justify my involvement as well. I told him that a couple of weeks earlier he had been arrested and that I had been working with an agent with the FBI out of Great Falls. As I continued explaining the details of the case, they all spilled out. I told him that the case was kind of high profile and that I was going to have to testify as a witness in his prosecution at Fort Lewis, outside of Seattle. Randy just sat there looking at me at first with a look of disbelief, and then the questions came.

Randy's jaw got very tight and he pressed his lips together. When he spoke, he raised his voice, saying, "How could you let this happen?" We talked more about the case, and I answered all his questions as best I could. But when it became clear that he was having a hard time processing what I was telling him, he stopped himself and said that we would talk about it later and that he needed time to think. I told him that I would just go home and when he was ready I would show him the case materials and news reports on the Internet. I left him at that point to fly his airplanes and was thankful at least that he had not reacted in a hostile or angry manner.

When we did talk, Randy made clear his fear that my involvement with Anderson would become public. He was also concerned about how people would react to learning about the case and my involvement. He asked if this would be a very public case or if it was going to be reported to any degree in the news. All I could tell Randy in response to his valid questions was what Mark had told me—that my identity and involvement would be guarded as closely as possible and that it was likely I would be able to complete my testimony as a witness in a closed-court setting. Randy's response seemed one of doom and gloom—a worst-case scenario in my mind. He said that he didn't see how this was going to be kept quiet or under the radar and that the media would then descend on Conrad and disrupt our lives. Worse, Islamic terrorists could learn of my identity and come after us. At the time, I didn't believe Randy's concerns would come to be and told him that his concerns were valid but added, "Don't fight me on this because I'm going to do it." However, in hindsight, Randy's words turned out to be prophetic.

I told Randy about the new FBI agent that I had been talking to, Agent Mark Seyler, and that we had a good rapport and I felt that he would look out for my interests as the case went forward. Soon after unloading about the Anderson case on Randy, I would introduce him to Mark, whom he would come to like and trust.

AS I SETTLED INTO SEAT 2-B on a little twin-prop plane, I felt a tightness in the back of my throat. Preflight stress, maybe. Fear of what would come next, for sure. I had raced through my morning routine—breakfast, shower, hair, makeup—but the airport security screeners had selected me for an extra "wanding," so of course I was the last passenger to board. I quickly shoved my briefcase under the seat in front of me and tried to calm myself, saying, "Take a breath, and this will pass." But my uneasiness only grew as the plane rolled down the runway at the Great Falls International Airport for its ascent up and over the Rocky Mountains. As the plane passed Mt. Rainier— a sight that is usually awe-inspiring and uplifting—I realized the inner turmoil I was experiencing this morning wasn't tension. It was dread.

My wanderings on the Internet had led me to more than a few dangerous fanatics. This work had landed me in the middle of one of the most dramatic court-martial cases in U.S. Army history. My two worlds, which I had struggled so hard to keep separate, were about to collide.

It was May 4, 2004, and I was traveling to the Fort Lewis army base, near Tacoma, for a so-called Article 32 hearing to determine whether Specialist Ryan Anderson would face a court-martial on charges of attempted espionage and attempted aiding the enemy— a terrorist group—during a time of war. The Army had decided in April that it intended to seek the death penalty should Anderson be convicted by court-martial for these high crimes against his fellow soldiers and his country.

I was harboring a lot of regrets at the moment. I regretted not keeping Randy better informed of what I was doing. I missed my children. But underneath all that, I was curious and slightly excited about experiencing an entirely new type of legal proceeding. I was also eager to see what my sacrifices and contributions in this case might actually mean for the security of my country.

In the months that had passed since I had encountered Anderson online back in October, I had often revisited the simple question "Why?" Was he inspired by the virtues and values of Islam, or the faith the Muslim people ascribe to it? Or was he inspired by something darker—something more heinous? Did he identify with the radical ideology of al-Qaeda to such a point that he felt compelled to engage in treasonous activities at the expense of his fellow soldiers and our country?

These were some of the questions that had been gnawing at me. At the same time, I was living my life. I was happy and content with my career, and as a wife and mother—my real world. I had been researching terrorism and infiltrating terrorist lairs on the Internet for over two years by this time. I felt a sense of reward and personal satisfaction knowing I was contributing to America's effort in the War on Terror—even if it was only in my own small way. But I also knew my secret needed to be protected.

Upon arriving at Fort Lewis, I was greeted by Captain Kimberly Cox, a member of the Judge Advocate General (JAG) prosecution team for the Anderson case, who secured my temporary pass and base ID. Captain Cox is friendly and polite, and we bonded quickly, which help to set me at ease. I was, however, apprehensive about meeting lead JAG prosecutor Major Melvin "Chris" Jenks. From our earliest telephone conversations about the case after Anderson was arrested back in February, we had clashed over the parameters of how my testimony as a witness in the Anderson case would play out.

No matter how or in what context I tried to explain to Major Jenks the concerns I had about being a witness in such a high-profile case involving terrorism, he remained unwilling to compromise. He passed my questions off as trivial or reactionary.

Captain Cox introduced me to the rest of the Anderson prosecution team, and most are calm and professional. Major Timothy McDonnell from the Pentagon's TCAP (Trial Counsel Assistance Program, which assists local JAG teams with high-profile cases) in Washington, D.C., and Captain Jennifer Barrett, who was also with TCAP, seem friendly and appreciative of my efforts in the case. I was also introduced to Specialist Skylee Robinson, the legal assistant to the prosecution team. And finally, I was introduced to Major Jenks. He was very formal and a bit impersonal, which didn't help my uneasiness.

A red-haired firecracker with a demeanor more like a drill sergeant than a lead prosecutor—at least any of the prosecutors I was familiar with—he took me aside to explain the process of a criminal prosecution and how a courtroom functions. I felt my annoyance rising. When he finished, I reminded him that I was a judge and ruled a courtroom of my own, so he didn't need to waste time educating me on legal proceedings.

It was clear from this point forward that Jenks and I would be on a collision course. His last statement to me at that first meeting was simply: "This is the trial of my career and I'm not going to let anything screw it up. Understand that this trial will not be about you." I was nothing short of offended, and wondered how I would ever get through this phase of the case. Seething, I assured him I had no preconceptions that this case was in any way about me and that I would do what was asked of me as long as I was treated with some respect.

After that, our relationship quickly deteriorated. Throughout my time at Fort Lewis, I found Jenks to be dismissive and disrespectful—not only to me but to his colleagues and everyone else. I hoped that his arrogance and ego would not undermine the case.

Later that first day at Fort Lewis, Jenks and the JAG team prepared me for my part in the hearing, which was like a preliminary hearing or grand jury proceeding in the civilian world. This was my first time as a witness, and I found it difficult. In all my years in the law, I had never really considered the pressure the process puts on a witness, or the range of emotions experienced. I was surprised to discover this about myself, and I kept wondering, "Why is this so damn hard?"

To make matters worse, Jenks continued to evade my efforts to clarify the conditions and parameters of my testimony. He clearly saw women as inferior and was fond of ordering others around. One afternoon, one of the women on the JAG team stormed into the office where I was sitting, reading a book while waiting to be summoned for my daily round of prep. She obviously didn't see me as she slammed the door behind her and exclaimed, "I wish someone would put anthrax in his coffee!" Of course I knew who she was referring to, and all I could do was giggle and say, "I hear ya!" She spun around, embarrassed. I told her not to worry; I wouldn't mention the incident to anyone. Relieved, she sat down with me for a few minutes, and we did a little venting.

Also to my annoyance, I was expected at the JAG building daily to be available when Jenks needed to do witness prep with me, but rather than simply picking up the phone and setting a time, I was left idle for hours on end with nowhere else to go. Some nights, I would not arrive back to my hotel room until 10:00 or 11:00, only to get up and go back to the JAG headquarters by 7:30 the next morning. I even felt a fleeting sympathy with Anderson, captured by a powerful government agency that was not interested in showing me any consideration or kindness.

After the first week of prep, Jenks decided that he and I simply couldn't work together, and he assigned Major McDonnell and Captain Barrett to finish preparing me for my testimony. Major McDonnell is a tall, soft-spoken man in his mid-forties with gray just touching the edges of his buzz haircut, as patient as Major Jenks is impatient. Still, I get along best with Captain Barrett, a sweetheart of a lawyer who is exactly my age, divorced, and now engaged to a Black Hawk pilot stationed in South Korea. When we tire of regurgitating testimony, she would sometimes talk about her wedding plans, which provided a blissful diversion.

This was a welcome development. During my ample downtime, I talked a lot to friends and family back home in Montana about my fears and concerns. My best friend back home, Chris Christensen—a true and virtuous prosecutor—served as the sounding board for my frustration with the military process. As always, he provided great insight and support.

My calls home to Randy and the kids were another source of comfort. Each day after updating Randy on the events of the day, he told me he was proud of me and to keep my chin up, and I would be home safe and sound in no time. We talked about the routines of home, the kids and school, and the things he was working on at the time. Still, my isolation and anxiety always resurfaced as soon as I hung up the phone.

As I had hoped, once I was in the hands of Major McDonnell and Captain Barrett, things went smoothly. We went through various techniques on how to best present the emails between Anderson and myself. They proposed different scenarios, and posed the questions they would ask, which was slightly confusing, since I had already memorized the emails in a certain order.

And then they tried to anticipate the questions I would get from the defense. Sometimes I tried to remember highlights from the emails, and what might have been going on in my personal life that day. I was, for example, very sick before Thanksgiving, shortly after our email exchanges began, and they were trying to prepare me for how that information could play into the defense's cross-examination. They even proffered questions about my possible motives.

"Isn't it true that you hate all Muslims?" Captain Barrett asks, playing the part of the defense attorney.

"No, it's not," I answer.

"Why is that?" queries Captain Barrett.

"Because I can separate the extremists from those who practice what the faith truly states, what the Koran is all about," I respond.

After just two days, they felt I was ready and that I should take the two remaining days before the hearing to relax and collect myself. I was to review my witness materials and email exchanges with Anderson, and we would meet at 6:30 the night before the hearing for a dry run. One important issue that we had not yet adequately addressed was my concern regarding security. I was told they would have answers for me that night. However, there was one last task to complete before I was done. I had to meet and be interviewed by Anderson's defense team and his lead attorney, Major Joseph "Jay" Morse.

Mid-afternoon on the last day of witness prep, Major McDonnell and Captain Barrett informed me that when we were done they would be taking me over to meet Major Morse. I had not had a lot of time to contemplate this process, which was probably good, since I had no time to get nervous.

I was numb and fatigued, to some degree just going through the motions at that point.

To my surprise, the meeting with Major Morse was not difficult. He seemed quite likeable and reasonable. The questions he asked were the kind I would expect of a defense attorney, and it took only three hours. At the conclusion of our meeting, he extended his hand and thanked me for my time and for being a witness in the case. I shook his hand, and without thinking, remarked how happy I was that he was more reasonable and personable than Major Jenks—immediately scolding myself afterward for such an unprofessional display.

I certainly wasn't going to mention to the JAG team what I had said to Major Morse. However, when Captain Barrett called me later that evening to see how my meeting with Major Morse had gone, I told her it was a relief to get that out of the way and that I was comfortable with the questions I had been asked. She seemed pleased, and told me to relax and to try to sleep. If I needed anything or had any questions before our meeting, she said, I should feel free to give her a call.

Hanging up with Captain Barrett that night, I finally felt that maybe this whole process wasn't as awful as I had perceived it to be. I called my friend Chris back home that night to get his input on what I had said to Major Morse about my feelings and opinion of Major Jenks. I was relieved to hear him say that he did not think it was a major blunder. That night, I got my best sleep yet in Fort Lewis.

The next day, I lay in bed thinking over everything that had led me here. Thoughts of how I could have done things differently so that I could have avoided becoming a witness came and went. I eventually resolved that the moment I took my information and materials to the FBI, I knew it was inevitable.

I found myself praying harder, and with a heavier heart, than I had in many years, asking God for the will and strength to get through this trying time in my life and to help me continue to do the right things for the right reasons. I was telling myself that my life and family back home in Montana would be exactly as I left it. I was not willing to consider that my life had changed permanently.

The day before the hearing seemed endless. I dutifully reviewed my witness materials. I tried to preoccupy myself with calming techniques and thoughts. All I wanted was to get the dry run done and get back to my room early for a long soak in the bathtub.

I arrived on base that night around 6:00 and swung through the Burger King drive-thru to grab a quick bite to eat before the dry run. I left my rental car and walked over to the temporary office that Major McDonnell and Captain Barrett had been using as their headquarters. I checked in and they told me to go ahead and sit in the office or the library and they would call me when they were ready. I remember looking at them, wanting to ask how long they thought I would have to wait, but I could see from their faces that they were under the gun, so I said that was fine and I'd have my cell phone on.

I decided to go to the library and use the Internet until I was called. By the time I arrived at the library it was close to 7:00, and I figured I'd be there only a short while. But by 8:00, my frustration was starting to surface. I thought, if they called right now we could be done by 9:00; I could be back at my hotel room by 9:30 and still be able to wind down and try to get some decent sleep. By 8:20, I was pissed off and decided to just head over to their office, since the library closed at 9:00 anyway.

When I arrived back at their office, there was no one there, and I thought, great, they forgot about me; now what do I do? I walked around the corridors of the building looking for McDonnell or Barrett and found them in a small courtroom on the first floor with documents and materials spread out all over the floor. When I asked if they were aware of the time, they both looked surprised that it was 9:00. They apologized, and I accepted, knowing full well what the night before any trial or hearing can be like.

We ended up going through my testimony twice, and things went well, but by 10:30 p.m. I just wanted to go to bed. That's when I asked about the security concerns. McDonnell and Barrett exchanged hesitant looks. They told me that Jenks did not feel that the level of concern I expressed regarding my security and that of my family merited the resolutions I had requested. I wanted to be able to testify in a closed-court setting outside the presence of the public attendees and media. I also wanted my undercover identity used in the case protected from any disclosure. I resented having my privacy invaded, especially since the one detail I had insisted on when I initially took the case to the FBI was that the government allow me to remain a confidential source.

My exhaustion was momentarily subsumed by rage. Barrett saw it, and told me she understood my concerns but that it was not a decision she or Major McDonnell had the authority to weigh in on. I didn't respond, just stood there cold as stone, as McDonnell advised me that I'd be expected at the JAG building the next morning at 7:00.

On the drive back to my hotel that night, I found myself suddenly crying. Once safely in my room, I started a bath and grabbed the cell phone from my purse and called home, desperately hoping Randy was still awake—though it was after 12:00 there.

There was no answer. Sitting in the tub and crying, I left a message telling him how much I was missing him and the kids; how scared I was and how I wished I could hear his voice at that moment. I told him I loved him and that if he happened to get my message before he got busy the next morning to call me first. I hung up and set my phone on the lid of the toilet, a perfect arm's length from the bathtub.

I lay back into the hot water with my eyes closed, willing myself to relax so that sleep would come. A few minutes later, my cell phone rang. It was Randy. The sound of his voice calmed me immediately. In all our years together, we had never been so far away from each other during such tumultuous times. I still felt his physical absence, but the sound of his voice was enough for the moment. By now it was after midnight in Washington, and we said our good nights to each other.

That night, sleep didn't come.

AT 4:30 A.M., I FINALLY DECIDED to stop trying. I turned on the local news, wondering if there would be any mention of the hearing. Just after 5:20, I heard the lady anchor say that the terrorism case for Army National Guardsman Ryan Anderson would begin that morning at Fort Lewis. She then tossed it to a reporter standing outside the gates at Fort Lewis, giving a rundown of the expected events. It felt weird to hear it on the news, and as I finished ironing my suit for the day, panic set in. Moments later, breakfast arrived, and I answered the door and picked up the courtesy copies of *USA Today* and the *Seattle Post-Intelligencer* provided by the hotel. As I had feared, there was an article in the *Post-Intelligencer* discussing the hearing, and as I scrolled through, I saw my name listed as one of the witnesses that day, but nothing else written about me. Though I wasn't happy, I figured that if that was the worst of it, I could live with it.

Running on adrenaline, I finished dressing, ate some scraps of the breakfast I had ordered, and made one last run at my witness materials before leaving the hotel.

As I entered the parking lot outside the JAG building, I noticed that I would not be able to park close to the building, as it had been barricaded off for the satellite news trucks that were starting to assemble. Then, as I approached the entrance of the JAG building after parking, I realized that I had left my temporary witness ID and base pass in the car. I cursed myself for having to walk back past the barrier, but if I didn't I wouldn't get inside the building without causing a fuss.

Luckily, no one seemed to notice me or care who I was. I passed through security and headed up to the second floor, where I was to meet Major McDonnell and Captain Barrett. I settled in on the couch and organized my materials, trying to look crisp and awake.

Captain Barrett was the first to greet me that morning. I remember being surprised that she was wearing her sand-colored fatigues and asked why she was not in formal military dress. Barrett explained that for proceedings such as an Article 32 hearing, officers were permitted to appear in their daily work attire; formal military dress was only required for events such as court-martial proceedings. She had to excuse herself and advised me that Specialist Skylee Robinson would be available to me leading up to my taking the stand that morning.

Soon, Specialist Robinson arrived to take me to the room where the witnesses would wait to be called. Robinson told me that Jenks had fixed the order of witnesses, and that I would be called first, so at least I would be done early and could rest and relax after that. Though I appreciated her efforts to reassure me, I was still fuming inside that not one of my concerns for security had been taken seriously by the Army.

As I entered the witness room, I had to pass through the media assembled outside, and was again relieved that no one seemed to notice me. I found a comfortable chair in the back of the room where I could be alone and observe the other witnesses. There were a few men there dressed in the same military fatigues as Captain Barrett. There were also several men in formal business suits. I had never met any of the Seattle FBI agents or personnel that had been involved in the case, but I had talked with Special Agent Troy Sowers a couple of times over the phone. I remember trying to pick out who he might be from the crowd of witnesses. I had been told prior to leaving for Fort Lewis that Agent Wilson would not be attending the hearing, because though he had been a liaison for me with the Seattle FBI, his role had ended there. So there were no familiar faces in the witness room that morning.

I decided to use my remaining time to go over my witness materials again. But before I could finish, Specialist Robinson appeared and summoned me. I grabbed my belongings and walked forward. She told me they were ready for me but that I could not take my stuff with me, so I handed it all over to her. She assured me she would keep my things with her and return them once I was off the witness stand.

As we made our way down to the courtroom, I was terrified. I remember the slightly irrational feeling that this must be what it is like to do a perp walk. I saw the doors to the courtroom open, and Major McDonnell beckon me forward. He whispered something I couldn't hear. As we passed the defense table, I stood within inches of Specialist Anderson for the first time. Prior to this moment, he had been known to me only virtually, and from the few pictures I had seen on TV and in the paper. As I raised my hand to take the witness oath, I noticed it was visibly shaking, and I willed myself to be calm. I sat erect as a fence post on the edge of the chair in the witness box. I crossed my legs tightly and held my hands together, making every effort not to look in the direction of Anderson.

Seated at the prosecution table were Major Jenks and Major McDonnell, surrounded by their files and binders. Seated at the defense table were only Major Morse and Anderson, who sat with head bowed in front of the blank yellow legal pad defendants use to communicate with their counsel.

In the gallery was an assortment of individuals. I assumed the people seated immediately behind Anderson were his friends and family, and that those seated behind the prosecution table were Army brass and officials. Sitting separate and apart were likely the media. I felt all their eyes fixed on me, wondering what my importance was to this case. Then I saw Major McDonnell rise.

McDonnell made a few comments to the court and then began his introductory questions. His approach was gentle and his voice was soft. I found myself answering his questions easily at first. But when they began to veer toward those related to my security concerns, I tried to be as vague as possible about my personal and professional life in Montana. At the height of my discomfort, I refused to answer questions regarding my family, my profession, and the undercover identity I had used in the case. I kept it up long enough for the judge to close the hearing to the public and media, allowing me to explain to him the extent of my concerns and the basis for those concerns. I was on my own now.

Of course, I had been down this road with both the prosecution and defense prior to ever taking the stand. I was willing to testify, but I wanted to do so as anonymously as possible where it concerned the media and public. I argued that Specialist Anderson's Sixth Amendment right to confront or cross-examine me would not be violated, because he had full disclosure of my background and the basis for my testimony. I simply wanted to protect my life and family to whatever extent I could.

In retrospect, perhaps I was just being difficult because no one had been willing to discuss my concerns previously. Either way, it didn't matter. I lost the argument, and the hearing was reopened, with all attendees reseated in the gallery. At this point, I knew I had to respect the decision of the court, and I tried to finish my testimony with as much dignity as I could muster.

I answered every question asked by Major McDonnell slowly and carefully, reminding myself to stick to the facts, not offer opinions, and that less is always more. As a judge myself, I knew how to control a witness and the extent of allowing relevant testimony, and decided I would apply those same points of control to myself. After all, I was the only one who could get me through this.

I finished McDonnell's direct examination. Then Major Morse's cross-examination passed, smooth and painless. The end was in sight!

My testimony as the first witness for Anderson's Article 32 hearing was done just before 1:00 that day. Though I had hoped to be able to return home to Montana the next day, Major Morse asked the court to hold me subject to recall as an essential witness to the case, and to proscribe that I remain at Fort Lewis until the proceedings concluded.

Jenks's team offered no objection.

Relieved I had made it through my testimony, I happily exited the witness box—not even contemplating what was waiting for me outside.

I COULD SEE I WAS ABOUT to be besieged, as I leaned and looked out the window of the JAG building. The media waited for me outside behind a barrier. I wished the day's events were a bad dream I could finally wake up from. But no such luck.

I had never spoken to the media before, and I was dazed by the fluffy white microphones that loom high above the heads of the reporters positioned outside in the parking lot. In that moment I knew that my desire to protect my life back home was naive, and that it would never be the same again. I knew I had to make my way to my rental car, but I was crying, scared. There were so many of them and then there was just me.

As I stood there staring out the doors of the building with tears running down my face, a guardian angel came to my aid. I felt a tap on my shoulder and turned to see a military policeman with a concerned look on his face. He asked what was wrong and if I needed any help. I remember replying, "I don't know . . . I don't know what to do," all choked up. He asked what the problem was, and I replied, "I can't get to my car without having those reporters and people behind the barricade coming toward me." I don't remember his name, or if he even offered it, but he said, "You're the witness in the Anderson hearing, right?" I responded that I was. He asked me if I would like him to walk me to my car, and I gratefully accepted.

He asked me where my car was parked, and I couldn't remember. He told me to give him my keys and stay close behind him as we moved through the madness. When we reached the media barricade, he put his arm out in front, waving them away as he plowed through, seemingly without effort. Though they shouted questions and snapped pictures, I tried not to look directly at them, hiding instead behind my guardian angel. Once we were clear of the throng, he pressed the alarm on my key chain so we could find my car.

When we reached it, I said I didn't know how I could ever thank him for saving me from the press, and he said, "Ma'am, you owe me no thanks. It is me who should be thanking you for saving my fellow soldiers from Anderson." Tears welled up in my eyes, and I told him how much it meant to hear that after all I had been through. He asked if I needed anything else, and I told him no, thanks, that now I felt safe. That was the last time I saw that soldier in person, though I have seen him several times in the television footage of our walk through the parking lot that afternoon.

Nothing that happened that day could have prepared me for the media onslaught—and everything else—that would follow.

BACK IN MY HOTEL ROOM, I sat on the bed, trying to process the day's events. I hadn't turned on my cell phone and didn't feel like talking to anyone at the moment. I didn't particularly want to know what was going on in the world, or even outside my hotel room. I was exhausted and my eyes burned from sleeplessness and tears. I grabbed the covers and pulled them close, but I don't remember falling asleep.

I opened my eyes just after 4:00 p.m., feeling like I had slept an eternity. I grabbed the remote and turned the TV on to Fox News. My eyes caught the news scroll at the bottom of the screen, and there it was. In an item about the hearing, it mentioned surprise witness Shannen Rossmiller, a judge from Montana, as the actual undercover party who had broken the case open. I slid up on my pillow and read the scroll a couple more times before flipping to the local news channels.

As I followed the coverage into the evening, I saw the footage of my walk with my guardian soldier, and the scared, pale look on my face. What little was being said about me and my part in the case was not unfavorable; I was just bothered by the whole situation.

I decided to wait to call home that night until I knew that Randy and the kids had finished dinner. But when I finally turned on my cell phone, I had six voicemail messages from Randy and Gail, my clerk. Apparently, around 3:00 p.m., the phone had started ringing, with various media people asking for the location of my hotel and my cell phone number to ask me for interviews. Thankfully, neither of them had provided any information on where I was staying or how to contact me. I was not ready to face them.

That night, Randy said, he stopped answering the phone altogether, letting the messages pile up on the machine. He was uneasy about this and upset with me for not calling home sooner to warn him. I told him I was so out of sorts that I hadn't wanted to call, and that I didn't think that they'd go as far as to call the court or my home. I explained that I had been put through the ringer that day and just collapsed once I got back to my room.

He said he understood, and asked me how the day had gone. I relayed as much as I could, including how my name had appeared in the news scroll. He turned to Fox News and confirmed that the scroll was still running. I told him that I wouldn't be coming home the next day, and in fact didn't know when I would be able to get home, since the judge was requiring me to remain through the Article 32 hearing. He wasn't happy about that, but he said that he understood. I briefly talked to each of the kids, telling them that things were fine and that I would be home soon.

After talking to Randy and the kids I was still exhausted, and opted to order something simple from room service and go back to sleep. Despite the harrowing events of the day, the reality of it all had not set in yet. I told myself that tomorrow I would be old news, as there would be other witnesses in the spotlight.

I slept for almost seven hours that night, which is highly unusual for me. I know I needed it.

I WOKE UP EARLY THE DAY after the hearing. I had not ordered any breakfast the night before and was starving. I decided to try to be positive, and to get a healthy perspective on my situation. When my breakfast finally arrived, I grabbed for the complimentary newspapers. What I saw there was totally unexpected.

Right there in the *Seattle Post-Intelligencer,* in black and white, were the facts and details I had testified to—information that identified not only me, but where I lived in Montana, the name and location of my court, and that I had three kids. I knew, as a judge, it was all fair game. But knowing that didn't help me swallow my fear. I was even more stunned to read what I had *not* mentioned in testimony—the name and details of the undercover identity I had used in the Anderson case. Right there, for everyone to see, was "khadija1417@hotmail.com." I could not fathom how the media had gotten this information. McDonnell and Barrett had insisted that Anderson's attorney, Major Morse, agreed that every email used in the hearing and entered into evidence that listed the names of the email accounts I had used to communicate with Anderson would be redacted, so that "khadija1417@hotmail.com" appeared as "xxxxxxxx@hotmail.com." Though the names by which we referred to each other within email exchanges were untouched, our online identities were supposed to be secret.

I simply couldn't believe it. I wondered if any of the other Seattle papers had printed my undercover identities. Since I didn't have a laptop with me, I'd have to go down to the business center of the hotel to find out. I didn't know whom to confront. More importantly, I wasn't sure how detrimental this disclosure would be to my communications with other jihadists in other ongoing cases.

I ate what I could of my breakfast and got myself to the computer.

What I found in the AP, *Seattle Times,* and *USA Today* was consistent with my discovery in the *Post-Intelligencer.* Anyone who cared to read it would now know that khadija1417@hotmail.com was not a radicalized male jihadist. Khadija was nothing less than a blond female judge who poses as a radical jihadist online in her free time.

The threats that followed, in the form of calls to my court and home, had a chillingly consistent message: we know who you really are and where we can find you.

SPECIALIST ANDERSON'S ARTICLE 32 hearing concluded on May 14, 2004. The presiding officer made the recommendation that there was sufficient evidence presented to require Anderson to face the five charges of attempted espionage and attempting to aid the enemy—a terrorist group—during a time of war, through a general court-martial, which is the most serious of the formal military trials. Included in the presiding officer's recommendation for a general court-martial would be the prosecution's continued position regarding its determination to continue the charges with the option to still pursue the death penalty.

With the hearing over, I was finally advised on the evening of May 14 that I was free to return home to Montana and that I would be contacted with return flight arrangements.

I had not talked to Major Jenks or Captain Cox about my deep concerns regarding my jihadist identity's disclosure and betrayal to the media. I figured I wouldn't get any answers from anyone until the hearing was over, so I resolved to wait to pursue the issue until that time.

CONSIDERING MY PREVIOUS DEALINGS with Major Jenks, I decided that Captain Cox would be the one I would reach out to in order to find out how and why my undercover identity had been disclosed to the media.

CHAPTER EIGHT

UNDER PROTECTION

Despite the fallout from the Anderson case, with public knowledge and attention also came many well-wishes, and the kindness that underlies who we are as Americans. I received emails, phone calls, letters, and other selfless gifts from people who appreciated my efforts and sacrifice.

Someone sent me an email saying, "I'd always wondered if there were people like Jack Bauer (24). This morning I found out you do exist." I was thrilled at this comparison, being an avid fan of the popular TV show. Another added, "You changed the paths of soldiers who would have died. Many funerals will not be held because of your tenaciousness." It was nice to receive these messages.

While I was away, I know Randy did his best to try to understand what had happened. He was as supportive as he could be. But in reality, the Anderson case marked a turning point for us, and we started fighting. In hindsight, it launched the downward spiral that would end in the eventual dissolution of our marriage.

I think Randy hoped, with good reason, that after the Anderson hearing I would quit my online work. But I couldn't, and I told him as much—hoping he would understand its importance and value. Even with everything that had happened, the work was a watershed for me personally. This was the first time in my life I was using all of my skills and talents, and the things that always made me "different," in a positive and rewarding way. I felt more competent, fulfilled, and engaged as a person fighting the War on Terror than I ever had before. Besides, shutting down would mean turning my back on soldiers and civilians and letting the jihadists win. I had seen firsthand the difference my work could make, and I simply could not quit, even if I had to tread more carefully than ever.

While I was still in Seattle, I had been contacted by Mike Carter, a reporter with the *Seattle Times,* who was among the media that attended Anderson's Article 32 hearing. He had approached me on the last day I was at Fort Lewis and asked if I would consider giving him an interview about how I had gotten into the world of online terrorism and the Anderson case, which I said I would consider once I was back home in Montana.

I found the media pretty exhausting throughout my stay at Fort Lewis. I know their intentions were good, but no one had taught me how to deal with them, and I wasn't sure to what extent I should. But they put the pressure on. Reporters found ways to follow me back to my hotel, trying to pull me aside to ask "just a few questions."

At first, I didn't realize that I could lay down terms under which I could give interviews. The turning point came when I discovered there were ways of controlling the message, and I decided that it might be in my interest to consider some of the interview requests. Rather than be frustrated and upset about the speculation flying around about me, I could set the record straight.

LIFE DID RETURN TO NORMAL in some ways when I got home. I was nervous about how people would react to the news, and to my Internet work. Other than my close family and friends, I had not bothered to tell anyone about the Anderson case. At first, perhaps naively, I hoped the coverage would remain local to Seattle.

For the most part, people were kind and appreciative, as well as curious. One day a Catholic nun from Seattle visiting family in the Conrad area stopped by my office asking to speak with me. She waited until I was through with my court duties that morning, then said she wanted to express her thanks to me for stepping up and doing the right thing in the face of personal sacrifice. At the moment I was still reeling a bit, and her kind words and wisdom provided me with the resolve to face the current reality.

While some people weren't sure what to say to me and avoided me, others took the time to approach me and offer their thanks and support. Some even asked questions to try to understand what I had done and why. I honestly appreciated those people who took the time to ask about the case and how I was doing, wanting to understand the circumstances. I'm sure to most people it was a little surreal. But back in 2004 we were not that far removed from the events of September 11, and the Iraq war was still fresh and controversial, especially those who had family members or friends in the military. Those in the military fold seemed to understand and appreciate what I had done more than others.

A few days after I got home, Mike Carter of the *Seattle Times* turned up again, asking if he could come to Montana for an interview. I had expected the media requests to subside by now, but they hadn't. I talked to Randy about it, since he was getting visibly annoyed with the requests, and I told him that maybe if I did one big print interview and addressed all the speculation and curiosity it would put an end to the calls. After thinking it over for a bit, he agreed. We decided that I would do the *Seattle Times*.

Within a day the details were set. Mike would come to Montana and interview me, but not Randy or the kids, and he had to agree to not reprint the khadija1417 identity. He was set to fly to Great Falls and drive up to Conrad the following week.

Then, on May 18, 2004, a suspicious call came into my court. Gail answered. The caller asked to speak with the woman judge, Shannen. He had a heavy accent and poor English. When Gail said I wasn't available, the caller told her to give me a message: "You tell her we know who she is now."

Gail immediately dialed *69 and wrote down the number. She Googled the area code and determined that the call had originated from the Toronto area. Other than the Anderson case, Gail was not aware of the specifics of any of my Internet work and had no reason to know what the caller's purpose was, but the broken English and heavy accent made her plenty suspicious. When I returned to work, she gave me the number she had written down and told me the call came from Toronto. Trying not to look scared, I thanked her and said I would give this over to Mark and the FBI and let them look into it.

That same day, the FBI ordered local law enforcement to put me under protection indefinitely.

As it would turn out, their concern was more than valid. The evidence Mark provided me indicated that the exposure of the khadija1417 identity had alerted my jihadist friends with GIMG that Abu Khadija was Shannen Rossmiller—definitely not the person that they believed they had been communicating and collaborating with. Apparently, the FBI, in conjunction with its Canadian counterpart, CSIS

(Canadian Secret Intelligence Services), would be watching the folks at GIMG for any further suspicious activity or threats to me. I received no other communications at the court or my home from any of the GIMG individuals, and the khadija1417 identity went the way of the martyrs.

From then on, I was terrified. Everything was in the hands of the FBI, and I had to trust Mark. I decided that under the circumstances, I didn't want to proceed with the *Seattle Times* interview, and called Mike Carter to cancel. This is where things went awry.

When I told Mike about the incident and the protection order, he said that he would do whatever he could to accommodate my concerns, but that he had already made his travel arrangements. He said he would be willing to consult with law enforcement to avoid making the situation any worse. Not reassured, I said I would consider giving him an interview sometime later when things had settled down. He responded that he'd just get on the plane and we could talk about it when he arrived. I felt things spinning out of control.

I spent the next couple of days trying to think of ways to avoid Mike and the whole situation, but I came up empty. He arrived the week of May 23. I dodged his calls, asking Gail to tell him I was busy with my court duties. Undaunted, Mike went around Conrad asking questions of various people who knew me to get background on who I was and what life was like in Conrad. One afternoon, he appeared in my courtroom and observed the hearings and appearances of the day. That's when I knew I was going to have to face him sooner or later. But the force of my own reaction surprised me. As soon as my proceedings were over, I excused myself to use the bathroom, where I panicked, ran out the back door of the building, jumped into my car, and sped home.

Randy was there, and I told him what had happened. I started crying, and then the phone rang. It was Gail, asking what the hell I'd done. She said she'd been talking to Mike and that he seemed nice and sincere about protecting me. Then, in her fantastically no-nonsense way, she told me to get my ass back down to the court and talk to him, as she couldn't entertain him all day. I knew that since I had set these events in motion, it was my job to see them through, so I picked myself up, reapplied my makeup, and went back down to the court.

I told Mike I was scared, and he said that he understood. He promised that if I gave him the interview, he would both respect my personal concerns and help me address the things I wanted to set straight with the public.

I had calmed down by this time and agreed to go forward.

The interview was not as difficult as I had imagined. He kept his word. Once he had the article drafted and ready to submit to his editors, he called me and read every word. The article came out on June 16, a front-page feature that continued on the back page of the first section. I was very pleased with how it turned out. However, my idea that it would somehow end the media interest was exactly wrong. Instead, what had primarily been newspaper and talk radio requests became national and network news shows, hounding me again at home and at the court.

But one incident that occurred as a result of the *Seattle Times* article was incredibly surreal, humbling, and flattering all at the same time. On the Friday before Father's Day, Gail answered a call from a gentleman on a tour bus from the Seattle area, taking a group of senior citizens through Montana. He said his tour group was diverting their route through Montana to come to Conrad and wanted to take me and my family out for dinner on Father's Day. I had already made plans to cook dinner for Randy and my dad that day, but there was no way I could turn down this thoughtful gentleman's offer.

I can hardly describe my feelings at the moment this huge tour bus pulled up outside the Durango Restaurant in Conrad. It took up half the block. And all of these senior citizens filed out of the bus. Each one was so sincere in greeting me, some even grabbing and hugging me. They were of the generation Tom Brokaw called "the Greatest Generation," and they confessed to me that in this day and age they didn't see people doing things for the greater good at a personal cost. They shared their stories of the war and life during it, and asked me lots of questions about myself and family, and why I had done what I had. As I watched the tour bus disappear, my eyes welled up with tears of appreciation. That was one of the favorite days of my life.

AT THE END OF JUNE, the Army decided to withdraw its desire to seek the death penalty for Specialist Anderson. This was something of a relief, because though I believe in the death penalty and its proper application when the circumstances of a case warrant it, I had privately struggled with how I might feel if Anderson were in fact convicted and sentenced to death. I had researched the Rosenberg case of the 1950s, another treason and espionage case. The first U.S. civilians to be found guilty of relaying U.S. military secrets to the Soviets, the married couple Ethel and Julius Rosenberg were subsequently sentenced to death. Their death sentence was controversial in that anti-Communist political climate. While there were those who supported their conviction, many Americans believed the death penalty was too severe for the circumstances of the case. Still, the Rosenbergs were executed in June of 1953.

The possibility that Anderson could be put to death was not something I particularly wanted on my conscience. I knew it was not a situation I had any control over, but I remember vividly my relief upon hearing the Army's decision. Not relief for Anderson, but for myself.

IN EARLY JULY, I RECEIVED my subpoena for the upcoming court-martial in the Anderson case, which was set to commence in late

August. I had been working with the JAG team off and on over the summer in preparation for the event. I spent many hours researching the court-martial process and reading as many legal cases as I could with similar underlying facts. After my experience relying on Major Jenks and the Army to prepare me for the Article 32 phase of the case, I decided that I was more than capable of preparing myself for the rest. The more I learned about the military court process, the more intrigued I became. If nothing else good comes out of this, I thought, at least I learned something entirely new.

BY EARLY JULY, I WAS GETTING calls from book agents and television and movie producers who had all kinds of pitches about how they saw my story and how it could be developed. I was not interested in the book, TV, or movie angles at the time, and joked with people that the last thing I wanted was to become the subject of a tawdry TV movie of the week. However, NBC News finally persuaded me to give them an interview that would air only after the Anderson court-martial had concluded. We discussed various terms, and finally settled on the NBC producers' coming to Montana for an interview. The whole process came together so quickly that I wasn't quite ready for it. When the day came, I lay in bed, fretting. Finally, shortly before we had agreed to meet, I pulled myself together and drove down to the Super 8 Motel. Though NBC correspondent Lisa Myers would be reporting the story, she would not actually be traveling with the news crew for the interview. I was familiar with Lisa Myers and her work and found her to be a strong and credible journalist. I was quite flattered that she would be the one I talked to. I knew I was in the hands of professionals who wanted to report a good and important news story, so it was in their interest to make me comfortable.

The whole crew was exceptionally friendly, kind, and patient. The whole process occurred over two and a half grueling days. We shot film in various locations around Conrad, including my courtroom, where they documented me performing various functions in my role as a judge. I dreaded the sit-down sections, since I had no idea how I would come across on a TV screen, but they kept assuring me that I looked fine and that I had answered their questions competently and well. In the end, I felt confident that they would put together a good story. I even felt like I had made three new friends.

So as long as nothing was misrepresented, I would be happy with the outcome.

In early August 2004, Specialist Robinson of the JAG prosecution team called to say that I would need to be out at Fort Lewis by August 22 and that the court-martial would begin on August 30. On receiving this news, I began putting my affairs with my court schedule and family life in order. This time around, the people in my life had a better understanding of the case, its importance, and the likelihood of more media requests. Randy and I had devised what we thought was a clever outgoing message for our answering machine: "You have reached the Rossmillers and we cannot take your call at this time. If you are a member of the media, please leave your name and contact information only once and we will return your call if we choose." People asked me back then why we didn't just change our telephone number and have it unlisted, but the simple reason was because Randy ran his computer business out of our home and all of his business calls came to that number.

I also told the people at my municipal court that, should any media requests come into the court while I was away, they should take the contact information and advise callers that only one call was necessary, and that if I chose to return their call, I would. All things considered, I felt I had prepared all of the important aspects of my life for my absence. If things became a circus again—at least we were somewhat prepared to deal with it.

THERE ARE THOSE JOURNEYS away from home that seem more like punishment than privilege. Fort Lewis, the second time around, was one such journey.

I was racked with anxiety and guilt about having to be gone for so long again.

I resented having my privacy invaded, especially since the one detail I had insisted on when I initially took the case to the FBI was that the government allow me to remain as a confidential source.

As it turned out, I would miss my kids' first day of school that year. We had done all the shopping for clothes and supplies before I left, so as not to inconvenience Randy any more than necessary. But it still made me sad.

I resented the fact that I wouldn't be there to fix my youngest daughter's hair before she leaves for school, or when my girls rush through the door to tell their stories about the first day back. I already knew that hearing it by phone wouldn't be the same.

I couldn't sleep the night before I left. I wondered if Anderson's mother would be in court this time, carrying her own memories of her son's first day of school. I tried to push such thoughts from my mind. Each time the mother in me bubbled up, I reminded myself that I was also a judge who dealt in facts, not emotions. I also reminded myself of what he could have done if he hadn't been stopped, and all the mothers who are still crying after 9/11 and the losses in Afghanistan and Iraq.

Hoping for sleep, I tried to divert my thoughts to something more benign. I mentally went over everything I packed earlier that night, ensuring I hadn't forgotten anything that I would need this time. One small comfort was the fact that my mom would be flying in from Reno to Fort Lewis to stay with me the weekend before the court-martial began. Though she couldn't stay for the first day, she would be there to pump me up and reassure me.

When it came time to say good-bye to Randy and the kids, I felt a huge lump in my throat. I was trying to keep my cool so the kids would not be upset; I wanted them to think of me as strong so they wouldn't worry about me. All I wanted them to do was enjoy their last days of summer vacation. Luckily, as I hugged and kissed each of them, I realized they were acting as though mom was just going on another trip. They had their little lives and the things that were preoccupying them, and I immediately realized that they were fine, and maybe I could let go of some of the guilt I was feeling about leaving.

Saying good-bye to Randy that morning was especially difficult, as I really wished there was a way he could come with me, but the task of keeping the home fires burning had to fall on his shoulders at that moment, and we couldn't afford to have him take time off. But Randy was strong and reassuring and kept telling me to just go and get it done, and that everything would be okay. I was go grateful he was there and willing to hold it all together.

Thankfully, the flight from Great Falls to Seattle is only about ninety minutes, so there wasn't a lot of time for me to sit and stew about things. I had purposely packed all of my witness materials in the bags that I had checked in at the airport so that I wouldn't feel obligated to review them. After all, there would be plenty of time for that in Fort Lewis. Instead, I pulled out my latest book—a Tom Clancy paperback, *The Teeth of the Tiger.*

When I arrived in Seattle, it was overcast and raining, which matched my mood. After exiting the plane and picking up my luggage at the baggage claim, I went over to check out my rental car. I had reserved a Pontiac Grand Prix, which was the same make and model of car I had at home, so that something would feel familiar. After standing in line and waiting and finally getting up to the counter, I was informed that they didn't have any Grand Prix cars available. Too downhearted to fight, I settled for a midsize Mitsubishi Galant.

Once I was settled in and unpacked, I called Captain Cox to let her know I had arrived safe and sound. We decided to meet the next morning at the visitor's center so that she could arrange for my base pass and ID.

I asked how prep was going for the court-martial, and she said it was going smoothly. She even reassured me that Major Jenks had been easier to work with and be around lately, so I might see some improvement this time. I told her I was happy to hear that and wondered if she had an idea when they wanted me to report to JAG for prep for the court-martial. She said that she didn't right then, but that she would find out and give me a call later.

For the next two days, I sat in my hotel room, waiting for a call, wondering who requested that I come early for trial preparation.

My hotel was near a beautiful wooded trail, but fear of missing a call as well as the nearly constant rain showers kept me from walking for very long. Instead, I spent most of those two days morose—lying in bed napping, watching TV, reading and reviewing the witness materials and email evidence I had amassed in the Anderson case.

It is difficult not to resent being taken away from my life and family for so much unplanned downtime. Of course, I'm generally in control of everything in my life. There was nothing about this case that I had any control over, which was very frustrating.

On Wednesday, August 25, I met with the prosecution team in the late afternoon. It was immediately clear that my earlier problems with Major Jenks were not to be resolved. He was as strong-willed and condescending as ever, raising the hairs on the back of my neck, it seems, even before he strode into the room. For someone who "commands" respect, Major Jenks had yet to win mine.

Luckily, most of my prep work was again with Major McDonnell and his assistant, Captain Barrett.

The next morning when I arrived back at the JAG building, everyone was busy, but the atmosphere seemed more organized and relaxed than it had the last time I was there. I told myself that this was a good sign and that I should try to leave the painful memories of the Article 32 experience behind and give this round a fair shot. Again, my mother's words of wisdom entered my mind—"wear your smile"; "kill them with kindness." Happily, I remembered that she would be with me soon.

I was done and free for the day by 2:00 that afternoon, and didn't really feel like just going back to my room and waiting or watching TV. Since I had never really seen the Seattle area before and didn't have anything else to do, I decided to just get in the car and drive and see where I ended up. I was excited to explore and get out of the hotel for a while.

I drove along the highway by the ocean and into Tacoma and downtown Seattle. I enjoyed watching the young punks hanging around the street. I remembered the case of the Green River serial killer, who murdered prostitutes he picked up along the Sea-Tac strip that I had followed with interest over the years. Gary Ridgway was arrested for the murders back in 2001, after a twenty-plus-year killing spree.

I decided to go sit in a Pizza Hut and wait for it to get dark enough so that I could see some of the seedy life that emerged along the Sea-Tac strip at night. I had seen prostitutes before in other big cities, and always wondered how life had led them there.

The next day I met with the JAG crew, and we went over the same materials and evidence that we had the day before, and no one seemed to have anything new regarding the case that I needed to know, so I was again done early that day, by lunchtime.

The weather was chilly and rainy, and I didn't feel like another driving adventure. Truth be told, I was feeling kind of lonely. I called Randy after I was done and on my way back to the hotel, and he was busy with work and the kids were not at home, so I left a message that I would call that night. At least my mom would be arriving the next day. I was excited to have someone to eat and talk with outside of the confines of my hotel room.

The rainy weather triggered my allergies, and I was constantly wiping my eyes. I could feel a sore throat and cough coming on. I figured some good sleep and resting my voice were in order.

Still, the mental exhaustion was wearing on me, and I wasn't eating or sleeping well. My hands and feet were beginning to swell. Then, I woke up the next morning with swollen glands, and my throat felt terrible. So when I ordered my breakfast that morning, I asked for room service to bring extra salt so I could gargle with salt water a couple of times to loosen things up. The salt water seemed to help a bit, but my voice was fading. Oh well, I thought, my mom's coming today, and she can step back into her role of taking care of me. The comfort and care of a mother can really never be replaced!

MY MOTHER WORKS AS A special education teacher in Reno during the school year, and travels back to Montana for the summers and vacations. She had just returned to Reno for the start of the fall session before I left for Seattle, and knew I was a nervous wreck about testifying. She had offered to come to give me at least a brief reprieve from the tension of the impending court-martial.

I was thrilled to see her when I saw her at baggage claim. As usual, she was impeccably dressed in Liz Claiborne jeans and a brilliant orange sweater that showed off her beautiful olive complexion and striking blue eyes. I was proud of how youthful and vibrant she seemed; not your typical granny. We hugged, and talked all the way back to the hotel.

In motherly fashion, she noticed I was more shaky than usual and was also concerned about my sore throat and the swelling in my limbs. She wanted me to go to a clinic, but there was no time. She reminded me to at least take deep breaths and calm myself down, since stress always aggravates my immune system.

I told her about the lack of progress in my personality conflict with Major Jenks. Somehow, I still didn't feel like delivering chocolate chip cookies to his door.

When my mom was finally settled into her room, she came over to mine and proceeded to check out all the clothes I brought and to inventory what she thought was appropriate to wear for the court-martial. I was thinking that some things never change, as I realized that part of her intent in coming was to make sure I would be properly dressed. Finally, she selected my tomato red dress suit, calling it a power suit. "That's all they'll look at," my mom said, meaning it would distract from any emotions I might wear on my face. "They won't even look at you."

U.S. Army policy made it impossible for my mother to join me on base for the prep sessions, which continued through the weekend. While I was away, my mother visited with cousins in Tacoma or read in her room. After a tedious day on Friday, we got away for a nice lunch at a local Italian restaurant, which, for me, included a several double-shot frozen daiquiris. I am not much of a drinker, but there are times when alcohol can take the edge off. I justified the daiquiris to myself and to my mother as being soothing for my sore throat, too.

I took my mother back to the airport on Sunday morning. Our time together was really minimal because of the schedule imposed by the prosecution team. But having her there centered me and reassured me that she was proud of me and knew I would come through for her. Mothers take care of their children, even when those children are cyber spies.

I hugged my mother, and tears came to my eyes.

"You'll be fine," she said. "You just have to remember to *not* overthink, overanalyze."

"I know," I answered, and, of course, I truly meant that. These were words I had uttered to my own children at difficult times in their lives. It is, however, easier said than done, and I hoped I could remember that the next time I tell someone else to do it. As I saw my mother to her plane, my isolation hit me hard. I fought the tears that I couldn't keep from falling.

THE FIRST MORNING OF THE court-martial, I felt stronger than I did at the Article 32 hearing. I was still scared and anxious, but outwardly holding my emotions together. When I first found out I was going to have to testify, I remember thinking, "Well, at least I'm familiar with the logistics." But it prepared me for nothing.

As a witness, I was very sure of my story, vexed when attorneys try to trip me up or cut off what I was about to say, and anxious to tell them things they didn't seem to want to hear. Judges can ask questions; witnesses only answer.

In truth, being a star witness in a high-profile criminal case has changed me as a judge, I know. In the months between the Article 32 hearing and the court-martial, I found I was more patient with witnesses. Now, when lawyers attempt to limit testimony, I am more lenient in allowing it to develop. I want to do more than just scratch the surface.

I arrived early on Monday, August 30, dressed in the tomato red suit my mother helped me select. Several people complimented me on it. My blond hair was blown dry and styled. I enjoyed the attention of the women on the prosecution team, since I didn't usually cause much of a stir back home in Montana. But today, I wanted to be taken seriously in every way. It was one of the most important moments of my life.

I entered the guarded witness room to wait. I was isolated from all the other witnesses this time. I had to take my escort with me every-where I went, even to the ladies' room! My escort was a nice young man, an Army Specialist from Oregon. When I knocked on the door of the witness room to ask if I could use the ladies' room, the Special-ist said, "Yes, ma'am, follow me." All of this made me uncomfortable, but there was nothing I could do about it.

About thirty minutes before I was to testify, the Specialist beck-oned me to follow him to security screening. I extended my hands to the latex-gloved security officer, who swiped them with a solution, then sent the sample through an explosive-detection machine. An alarm went off, but I was oblivious; it couldn't be me.

Then the security officer approached me.

"We need to re-test you," she said.

Again, I put out my hands, and again, she swiped them, only to have the alarms scream one more time. Suddenly, more security per-sonnel appeared out of nowhere, then disappeared into another room. No one was talking to me.

"What happened?" I asked.

Instead of answering, the one officer still present shrugged her shoulders.

A few minutes later, a female security officer returned with one of the female specialists for the prosecution team. They asked me to accompany them into the next room.

I was too confused to argue. I followed the officers to a room off the screening area and listened, in disbelief, as they explained that I will now undergo a strip search.

"You have to be kidding, right?" I asked, laughing.

"No," one security officer said. "We're not."

I was laughing again, from shock. They, however, were not.

I extended my arms and widened my stance in preparation for the pat-down that has become standard procedure for high-risk passengers about to board an airplane, and thought that would be it. "Now we need you to step out of your dress and your bra," said the security officer.

"WHAT?" I responded, horrified.

"We need you to . . ." she began again.

"NO," I answered, interrupting her sentence. "I CAN'T do that."

"If you don't comply, we will get a court order to compel you," she said.

"Damn," I said to myself. I said nothing to them.

Tears were brimming in my eyes. I felt so humiliated and belittled as I removed my power suit, feeling much less powerful now, and the bra beneath it. It was a personal low point. I kept hoping I would wake up from this dream and my life would be as it was before February of 2004. Instead, I was standing, nearly nude, in front of two strangers, and within shouting distance of a packed courtroom.

The security officers found no hidden explosives, or guns, or pipe bombs on my person and allowed me to re-dress and return to the security area to wait for my call to the stand. My tears dried. I was silently praying for every bit of strength I could muster to get through this ordeal. I ordered myself to dismiss what had just happened, and tried to concentrate, instead, on what lay ahead.

Even though I had not been in the courtroom, I knew the first person on the stand was a former New York City fireman named Scott Spect who had trained with Anderson in boot camp shortly after 9/11. He was testifying that, even before my discovery, Anderson had vocalized support for the enemy, and that he had even alerted their company drill sergeant. For example, when Spect asked him how he felt about 9/11, Anderson answered, "You people have a problem."

After Spect left the stand, we met briefly in the hallway. He grasped my hand.

"It's an honor to meet you, ma'am," he said.

I shook his hand and answered, "You take care of yourself over there."

I was speaking of Iraq. He was shipped out with his unit just three weeks later.

Then I turned, back straight, and walked into the courtroom.

It had been remodeled since I was last there, in May. Situated on the third floor of the red-bricked JAG building, the courtroom itself was smaller than my own back in Conrad. It had been repainted in a calm brown tone, and maroon carpet had been added to the floors, softening the starkness I felt during the Article 32 hearing.

There were four rows of seats for observers behind the counsel tables, and desks near the judge's bench, as well, for the bailiff and court reporter. Off to one side was the officers panel box.

In a court-martial, defendants are allowed to choose between a jury of their peers, meaning U.S. Army personnel of similar rank, or a jury of officers. Anderson chose a panel of officers. It was a diverse panel of nine, three females and six males, several of whom were of African-American or Hispanic descent. There were majors and captains, and a colonel. The lowest rank was a lieutenant.

There was legal strategy, I knew, in selecting officers versus enlisted men as jurors. Since Anderson stood accused of attempting to divulge information that could have harmed the troops actually fighting in Iraq, his defense team probably assumed he would be better off with officers rather than enlisted men and women who might have been among those wounded or killed had his plan succeeded. It was, of course, too soon to tell whether this strategy would actually play in his favor.

Anderson was wearing his Class-A formal uniform. His black boots were shined, his hair was cropped close to his scalp, and his wire-rimmed glasses were pushed back on his nose. His head was down, and he was scribbling on a pad as I walked by the defense table. We didn't share a glance, although I sensed the current between us.

Colonel Debra Boudreau, the hearing officer, watched as the clerk asked me to place my hand on the Bible and swear to "tell the truth, the whole truth and nothing but the truth, so help me God." For a brief second, the irony of me swearing on a Bible before a defendant who believes only in the Koran flashed through my mind, but I quickly focused on the prosecution team, who were about to begin their questioning.

I felt myself starting to shake but controlled it by sitting up very straight, like I had a board against my back, and pressed my hands together in my lap.

Colonel Boudreau asked me a question about the difference between civilian courts versus what was going on in her court.

"What is your understanding of these proceedings?" questioned Colonel Boudreau.

I smiled and chuckled before answering.

"I wish we had the same system on the civilian side as you do on the military side when it comes to criminal justice. It really, frankly, runs much more smoothly," I said.

I made eye contact with Anderson for the first time when the prosecution asked me to point him out. At the Article 32 hearing in May, he never looked at me. This time, he glances up, his ice-blue eyes meeting mine for a second. His expressionless gaze was unnerving. I clasped my hands together even tighter.

I had, of course, prepared for the questions from the prosecution over and over. I found that I was surprisingly calm and controlled in my answers. Our hours of prep had paid off, and I breezed through without a slip-up. There was only one question that truly took me by surprise.

"When you were exchanging emails with Anderson, did you ever think there would be an arrest and a court-martial? How do you feel about being responsible for that?" asked one of the prosecution team.

When he said the word "responsible," I paused, knowing there wouldn't be a quick answer. It was actually something I had talked about with Randy, but I was still slow to respond.

"No, I never thought it would get this far," I said. "The only thing I ever really intended was, if this person was in the military, and if he did have these intentions, I figured it would end up in the right hands and the military would take care of it."

Unlike my courtroom in Conrad, the officers panel of jurors here were also allowed to ask questions. I was supposed to look at the panel every time I answered a question, which was also intimidating. I moved my eyes from face to face, watched as they jot down notes, and nodded slightly when a question was asked.

One of the officers asked me about a graphic on the Brave Muslim website. "What does it signify?" he asked.

"Every time al-Qaeda takes responsibility for an operation or an attack," I replied, "they make a movie or some sort of graphic sign. The al-Qaeda graphic on the Brave Muslim site was one they had made up for the bombings in Tanzania and Kenya in 1998, the embassy bombings. The significance is that any website on the Internet that sympathizes with al-Qaeda or is al-Qaeda affiliated puts up these graphics. It is how they show their support. It's like a badge." I watched them nod once again in understanding.

Even as I spoke, I am aware of Anderson's family sitting in the four rows behind the defense table. When the prosecution paused to study a document, I caught their eyes. It was so hard for me to watch the agony of Anderson's young wife, Erin, and his parents. Erin, a pixie of a girl, was quietly crying, while Anderson's father, Bruce, was attempting to comfort her. This time his mother, Linda Tucker, was present as well. Her pain was evident in her eyes. Internally, I struggled. I wished I could tell them that while I am sorry for my part in their sorrow, I was not sorry for turning him in. I hoped that someday they would understand.

The defense attorney rose to begin his cross-examination, and I was surprisingly calm. I knew that much of my serenity in the face of his questioning stemmed from our meeting the Saturday night prior. It was then, for the first time, that I could vocalize my concerns about some of the information he wanted from me: all my online identities and contacts. I explained to him how divulging such information would jeopardize my safety and the safety of my family, and told him of the threatening phone call that came into my clerk's office shortly after the Article 32 hearing, when a newspaper reporter printed my online identity.

Major Morse agreed that the information he had requested was not relevant to the case, and told me he would not press the issue further. He also said that, had he known the basis for my concerns, we could have avoided the struggle over the summer. I left his office even more furious at Major Jenks, who had clearly never believed my concerns were relevant enough to even explain them to Major Morse.

I remember my conversation with the prosecution team after our meeting.

"We were able to come to an understanding that the things he was requesting, like the online IDs, weren't applicable to this case," I told them.

"Yeah, well, we'll see" was Major Jenks reply.

I took great satisfaction in answering all of the defense's questions, none of which relate to my other identities.

As I exited the courtroom, excused for the day after nearly five hours on the stand, a male security guard took my arm and asked me to come with him. I followed him out of the JAG building to where my silver rental car was parked in a lot on the far end. I saw a white van stopped near my car, and officers dressed in masks and helmets, with dogs on leashes, circling it.

"Who has had access to your car?" asked the security officer.

"I don't know," I answered.

"Have you been followed or noticed anything unusual?" he queried.

"I don't think so," I said.

"Do you know of anyone who would want to harm you?" he asked.

"I don't know," I said. "WHAT is going on?"

It is then that I found out that the reason dogs were sniffing around my car was because of explosive residue on the door handle and trunk!

I IMMEDIATELY CALLED MARK. As it turned out, he was ten miles out of Conrad, driving back from Shelby, a town twenty-five miles north. He pulled over to the side of the road to talk to me and told me to take some deep breaths and try to calm down so that he could get the whole story from me and decide the best way to help. As I relayed what had happened that morning and with my rental car, he said he would contact the Seattle FBI office and have someone come down to Fort Lewis and try to sort things out. I was only able to talk to him for a few minutes when Captain Barrett and another woman I didn't recognize walked up to me indicating that they needed to talk to me. The last thing he asked before we hung up was if Randy knew what had happened, and I told him that I had not had time to call him yet, and he offered to go into Conrad and talk to Randy. God bless that man, I thought. I don't know how I would have gotten through any of it without him.

When I got off the phone, Barrett introduced the woman with her as an agent with DHS in Seattle, who had come down to the base after they found explosive residue on my hands earlier that morning. She advised me that they had sent agents to my hotel to collect my belongings and would return them once they had been searched and they determined that there was no threat. She also advised me that they were moving me to another hotel away from Fort Lewis, in Tacoma.

I was becoming angrier by the second. The first thing I asked after she stopped talking was whether there was a search warrant authorizing any of these actions—the search of my car, my hotel room, my personal belongings? No, she answered coldly. Apparently, they felt that the fact that I had triggered the bomb detection machine twice that morning was sufficient to allow them such liberties. I defensively replied that, had anyone bothered to simply ask me for permission to search my car, hotel room, and personal belongings, I would have given my consent, but the fact that no one had even thought to give me that simple courtesy was outrageous. Though I was the Army's witness in this case, at no time had I waived my constitutional rights, especially regarding an unauthorized search and seizure.

Again, I had no choice in this matter, just as I had been given no choice about anything in this case. To make things worse, the media was camped out in the parking lot, taping video of the bomb squad and dogs sniffing around my car! At that moment I couldn't imagine that anything could get worse.

On the way to my new hotel in Tacoma, I called Mark again to advise him of the agents at my hotel searching my room and personal belongings, and that they were moving me to a new hotel. He was perplexed, asking me if there was any way I had come into contact with any explosive materials or even gunshot residue. I told him that there wasn't. He asked me if I had noticed any suspicious people or activity around me over the last couple of days. Had I been followed? Could I remember anything now that might seem out of the ordinary? Nothing, I answered. He told me that after all the turmoil of the day had settled down, something might trigger my memory later, so I should try to keep reviewing the last few days in my mind. He told me that he had talked to the Seattle FBI office and that they would be sending someone up to Fort Lewis that afternoon and he would update me later when he knew more.

My new hotel was a Holiday Inn Express right in the middle of downtown Tacoma. Not the best or safest surroundings, but at that point all I wanted was to get away from it all and lock myself in my room. My personal belongings were not returned until early that evening, so I had been stuck in my dress suit all day, making it hard to unwind. If there is anything I loathe, it is feeling helpless, and I had never felt more so.

When I spoke to Randy later that night, he told me that Mark had come to the house in the afternoon and told him everything, but he hadn't heard anything new since then. I was not in the mood to relive the day's events, and thankfully Randy understood. I didn't even want to turn on the TV and see what had been reported about the court-martial or the bomb squad incident that night. I simply wanted to forget it all.

The next morning, I woke up around 4:30 and decided that sooner or later I was going to have to face the news. I flipped the TV on to Fox, and lay there trying to decide if I was hungry or not. I hadn't eaten dinner the night before, so normally I would have been ravenous, but not today. The breaking news of the morning was that President Clinton had been hospitalized for an emergency heart procedure and that then-Senator Hillary Clinton was traveling to New York City to be with the former president.

I had always liked Bill Clinton and admired how he traversed through life, even if I didn't always agree with his politics. Though I was sad to hear of his health crisis, I was quietly hoping that this news would trump any news about the court-martial. And lo and behold, there was little more than the typical cursory report that the court-martial was under way and a rundown of the charges against Anderson.

Around 7:00 p.m., I turned to one of the local Seattle news channels. Here, we were front and center. There was mention of me and my testimony, but also other witnesses who had testified later in the afternoon. I kept waiting to hear a report of the bomb scare, but nothing came. "How can that be?" I thought. Nevertheless, I was relieved. I just hoped it would stay that way.

Two more days would pass while I waited out the court-martial in my hotel room. I felt like I might be sliding into a depression. I had no energy, appetite, or desire to do anything. I didn't even feel like calling home to talk to Randy and the kids. I forced myself to do it each day, despite having no news to report. Randy would tell me each day what media had left messages, and I had no interest. I felt like my life was no longer my own. I didn't feel appreciated or proud; I felt overlooked and violated. I lay in bed for such long periods of time over those two days that I developed a terrible headache that I couldn't get rid of. Simply put, I was miserable.

The next morning, September 3, media outlets were reporting that the Army expected to wrap up the court-martial that day, with closing statements in the afternoon. Hearing this news, I thought, "Isn't it just like the Army to forget they dumped me in downtown Tacoma and didn't bother to tell me I would no longer be needed?" However, when I checked the messages on my cell phone, there was a message requesting that I come back to the proceedings later that morning. Since anything sounded better at that point than simply existing in my hotel room, I got myself dressed and presentable, and I arrived back at Fort Lewis around 11:30.

At the JAG building, I tried to park my car away from the media still camped out in the lot. I had my raincoat with me, and though it was not raining that day I put the coat on and covered my head with the hood as I walked up to the building. I got through security without incident. I was a noticeable figure at the JAG building by this time, and once I was inside everyone I passed knew who I was and said hello.

It didn't take long for Specialist Robinson to find me and take me aside. She updated me on how the proceedings had gone over the last couple of days and was kind enough to ask if I had recovered from the turmoil of the first day. I told her that I was fine, just glad that things were coming to an end. For the first time since I had met her back in May during the Article 32 phase, Robinson told me that she was so thankful for what I had done with this case, because she had been set to deploy to the same place as Anderson and his unit—the Army's

Balad Air Base in Iraq. I asked her why she had never told me that, and she said she didn't know but that now that things were wrapping up and this case would be over she wanted to make sure that she made an effort to thank me. I was very touched, and it triggered the well of emotions I had been repressing over the last couple of days, so that I had to take a few minutes to compose myself.

Specialist Robinson also advised me that after the lunch break the parties would be doing their closing statements, and I should be present in the courtroom. She had listened to Jenks practice his statement the night before, and she said no matter how I felt about him, it was powerful and she knew I would appreciate hearing it. I told her I wanted to get something from the vending machines, as I was finally feeling an appetite creeping back. She said that when I got back she would escort me into the courtroom so that I would have a good seat.

Seeing the dreaded explosive detection machine, I made sure to wash and scrub my hands hard before returning to the courtroom. As I presented my hands to the MPs doing the hand swabbing, they smiled at me, and one said his fingers were crossed that I didn't set the machine off again and cause an international incident. Thankfully, I passed the swabbing tests and was able to slip into the courtroom without any fanfare. I was seated in the middle of the second row, almost directly behind the defense and prosecution counsel tables. I had brought along a book, not knowing what to expect that morning when I left my hotel room, and now I was glad for the diversion it provided. I was uncomfortable and nervous but trying not to look it.

The courtroom began to fill again. I noticed that the media filed into the last row of seats, while military personnel sat closer to the front. One Army officer who had been taking notes while I was testifying on Monday sat on my right side, and the Army officer Ricardo Romero, who had posed as the undercover al-Qaeda operative at the

Anderson meetings back in February, sat down on my left. I smiled at both men, who said hello and asked how I was doing. The last people that I noticed entering the courtroom were Anderson's parents and wife, who also sat in the same row as me.

Major Jenks entered, going directly to the counsel table and shuffling some papers, while I tried to appear deeply entrenched in my book. Then I saw him coming toward me. I immediately got nervous. As he approached me, he said, "Ms. Rossmiller," and I looked up at him and closed my book. "I am sorry you had a difficult time on Monday, but you were fantastic on the stand. I wanted to tell you how much I appreciate all you did to get us to this point in the case." The look on his face appeared sincere, and I felt a pang of guilt for harboring the anger I had and fixing him as the target of my resentment. At the same time, I was shocked. I said, "Thank you, Major Jenks. It means a lot to me to hear that from you." I told him that I heard he had prepared a very powerful closing and was looking forward to hearing it.

As Jenks turned to leave, I had a roiling sea inside me. I considered leaving the courtroom but decided that was not an option because I would have to walk by Anderson's family, who I assumed wanted nothing more than to shove daggers in my back. I was stuck. I realized my role as a witness had shifted to that of observer, once again helpless to change the outcome of anything.

At that moment Colonel Boudreau entered the courtroom from chambers and took her seat on the bench. Next, the officers panel filed into the jury box and were seated. Boudreau asked counsel if they were ready to proceed with closing statements, and both indicated that they were. Major Jenks stood up and began.

He summarized the case for the officers panel, pointing out the elements of each offense they were charged with considering. He focused on Anderson's intent, pointing out that Anderson was clear about all of it in the text messages and emails he exchanged with Shannen Ross-miller and in the meetings with the undercover agents. Finally, he said, the best evidence of Anderson's intentions was the undercover video-tape of his meetings with the undercover agents. All the evidence sub-mitted and entered by the government against Anderson clearly showed the information he was willing to share with al-Qaeda.

In Anderson's defense, Major Morse asserted that the government had not proved beyond a reasonable doubt that Anderson intended to help al-Qaeda. Morse passionately claimed that Anderson's larger-than-life ideas, actions, and ramblings were all indicative of his manic depression and Asperger's syndrome. Morse further claimed that An-derson wasn't asserting that he didn't know right from wrong, just that he wasn't always able to properly distinguish them in social situ-ations. Morse wrapped up by stating that based on all these factors, Anderson was incapable of the criminal intent required for the panel to find him guilty.

With a measure of passion and resolve I had never seen in him before, Jenks, in his rebuttal statement to Morse's closing argument, loudly urged the panel not to buy what Morse was trying to feed them. He claimed that Anderson's defense amounted to nothing more than an attempt to shield the panel from the "real" Ryan Anderson, a calculating person with no empathy for others who had severely jeop-ardized his fellow soldiers and wished for their deaths at the hands of al-Qaeda. The only person Ryan Anderson cares about, Jenks al-leged, is himself. To prove his point, Jenks showed a portion of the undercover video documenting Anderson telling the Army undercover agents that he was a tank commander and carefully explaining how to damage the M1-A1 and M1-A2 Abrams tanks, take them over, and kill the crews inside.

Jenks finally closed his rebuttal at around 6:00 p.m., by asking the panel to "see Amir Abdul Rashid for what he is," referencing the name Anderson used in communications with me and on extremist websites. Jenks also urged that the panel see Anderson as "a traitor. A traitor who betrayed our country, a traitor who betrayed our Army and a traitor who betrayed our fellow soldiers." When he finished, you could have heard a pin drop.

The case was left in the hands of the panel, and I wondered how long they would deliberate. I spent that afternoon talking with the people I had come to know over the last six months. I enjoyed listening to Captain Barrett talk with excitement about returning home to D.C. and seeing her fiancé, and their plans for their upcoming wedding and honeymoon. After a couple of hours, though, I wanted to be alone, and decided to take a walk outside. At that point, I didn't care if the media snapped pictures of me or not. I knew the end was in sight. Suddenly my cell phone rang. They had reached a decision. The officers panel had deliberated for just four and a half hours.

It occurred to me that none of us would be there had it not been for me. Was that good or bad? I couldn't decide.

The verdict was guilty on all five counts.

At that moment I glanced over to Anderson's family and saw his parents gasp. I also noticed his wife was crying.

I sat, stunned, and then started to cry myself. Covering my mouth, I said out loud, "Oh, my God, what have I done." The Army officer sitting to my right gently put his arm around me and said, "You may have just prevented the deaths of a whole lot of soldiers. You did the right thing. He could have been another Timothy McVeigh." I remember looking at him and saying, "I don't know how to feel about all of this, but I appreciate your kind words."

After the verdict was read, Colonel Boudreau advised the officers panel that they were now charged with making their recommendation for sentencing.

Once the officers panel left to deliberate again, it was late, almost 10:00. I was tired and I felt like being alone. It was time for me to start the process of moving on with my life.

The next morning I awoke to the news that Anderson would spend life in prison for his treason. I think I was both happy and sad at the same time. I cried then, for Ryan Anderson, and maybe a little for myself.

With everything that was going on, I had almost forgotten that the television interview I had done with NBC was airing that next morning. I was so numb inside that it was surreal to watch myself on TV. I thought that it wasn't that bad, and I was happy with how Lisa Myers had reported the story.

That morning after Anderson had been convicted, I made arrangements to go home. As I was packing up all of my stuff, my cell phone rang. It was a producer at *Good Morning America,* telling me that the show wanted to bring me to New York to be interviewed by Charlie Gibson about the Anderson case. I told the producer that I was just packing to head home, but that I would call him back in the next day or so and let him know what I decided.

Going home had never felt so good. It felt different this time, since I could finally relax into a sense of pride about the case and what I had done. I wasn't just home; I was home free.

I had told Randy while I was waiting to board my flight home that *Good Morning America* had contacted me about coming out to New York to be interviewed and that if he wanted to he would be able to come with me. I told him to think about it and we could discuss it when I got home. As for Randy and me, I thought it might be good for us to get away and for him to experience something with me instead of us always being apart.

Partially for this reason, I agreed to do *Good Morning America* in person at the show's Times Square studio, but only if they would have me there for the third anniversary of 9/11. Specialist Anderson was convicted by court-martial on September 4, 2004, only a week before. I had not been to New York since my high school trip, so I jumped at the opportunity. Since we didn't have the money to fly there ourselves and stay at a hotel (except for travel and hotel, only our expenses were covered for meals and taxis), I was able to work out a deal with the producers to stay three nights and four days, giving me the chance to see the site that I felt so connected to. Charlie Gibson was very sweet, saying, "We don't normally break the bank for guests! But bringing you here in person is important."

I honestly wasn't looking for more publicity, because I just wanted to go back to my life and family. But the constant requests for interviews about the Anderson case eventually convinced me that there was some value in explaining to my fellow Americans what I had done. Even more important, I thought it might serve to close that chapter in my life. I felt that the danger people like Anderson represented to our country could not be underestimated, and I was in a unique position to convey this.

I also needed to see Ground Zero. To me, it's a sacred site. I was so nervous, heading downtown in a yellow taxi, two days before the anniversary. As we got closer and closer, I recognized the names of the streets that had been affected.

Once the taxi arrived at the site, Randy and I got out and began walking around.

I couldn't believe it was still just a giant hole. Then I went and I stood in front of the readers who were practicing calling out the names of the victims. Some of the names I recognized by now.

My hair had been down for my TV appearance, and now I put it up in a ponytail. I was no longer wearing the red suit I wore on the show. Suddenly, I felt a tap on my shoulder, and there was a CNN camera crew and a reporter who said, "I saw you this morning," recalling my role in the Anderson case. How the heck she picked me out of the crowd, I don't know. She asked, "Why are you down here?" and I told her. She then asked if I would go on camera. I knew if I said no, she would just follow me around until I conceded. So I agreed, and she asked again on camera why I was there.

I said, "Years ago I was up in those towers." I went on to explain that this was a spiritual thing for me and that I needed to see it for closure. After she left I just sat there. I didn't know what to think or feel. I just knew I wanted to be there. It was so huge. The vastness was unexplainable.

To me 9/11 is a special holiday, a day I do not work but instead pay my respects to those who died. I would hope that someday it will officially become a national day of remembrance. As it turned out, I was wrong about the closure part. I couldn't move past 9/11 after my visit. It became even more my appendage.

A journalist who interviewed me for the *Philadelphia Inquirer* asked a therapist why he thought I was still so transfixed by 9/11 and couldn't seem to, as he put it, "move on." The therapist told him that people re-victimize themselves over and over until they reach resolution. That makes sense to me intellectually. But how can there be resolution in the War on Terror, when the next chapter could open anytime?

CHAPTER NINE

A BLACK FLAG

Unfortunately, there was one aspect still unresolved after the Anderson case. I was harboring a lot of hard feelings about some of the members of 7Seas, and after the court-martial, there was plenty of infighting, resentment, and misunderstanding to go around.

Because I had mentioned the case to some of my colleagues in 7Seas, they had provided cursory input and assistance. I sincerely appreciated each person's expertise and all they individually brought to the table. But after Rogue's attempt to claim credit for the case, things spun out of control. The case and its aftermath had disrupted my personal and professional life to the point that I had to make some painful decisions.

Now that I had been outed and there was broad public awareness of the work I was doing, if I wanted to avoid another chaotic mess like the Anderson case, I realized I would have to have a formal relationship with the FBI.

Prior to the Anderson case, I hadn't had one agent designated as a point of contact with the FBI other than Special Agent Wilson in the very beginning. I wasn't interested in a formal relationship at that point because I was a sitting judge and I wanted to keep my Internet work separate from my personal and professional lives. That all changed after the Anderson case.

I obviously didn't want to stop my Internet work, and I was still providing useful and valuable information to the FBI. So it made sense, from their perspective as well, to assign someone to work with me in a more formal and consistent manner after the Anderson case.

I decided that in order to continue in a focused way, I would have to ensure my family was protected. I was also going to have to part ways with 7Seas because, as Mark explained, the FBI couldn't work with an entire group spread across the globe. It simply presented too many possibilities for things to go awry. This was not a great loss, since I had come to realize that things had changed so much that working with the remaining members of 7Seas would not be feasible, anyway.

Still, it was a painful decision. I had developed friendships that I treasured. Each of the members of the group had their own unique expertise, talents, and skills, which made for a shared a collection of strengths, when there wasn't internal fighting among the group. It was an entirely new approach to tackling the terrorist enemy that we all wanted to see defeated. But the lack of cohesion ultimately doomed it.

I know that, even today, some former members of 7Seas have a hard time understanding my decision to leave. I tried to explain my dilemma reasonably, knowing there would be hard feelings no matter what. When I left 7Seas after the Anderson court-martial, there was still a level of cohesion in the group despite the mistrust that had materialized after my departure.

EARLY IN THE MORNING OF Sunday, December 5, 2004, my newfound serenity was shattered when two city police officers came pounding on my front door and ringing the bell repeatedly. When I answered the door, their eyes were wild and wide, and they seemed shocked to see me. The female officer, Amanda, said, "Oh, thank God, you are alive!" I was utterly perplexed at their urgency, still bleary with sleep. They asked me where my car was, and I told them the garage. It was then they asked to come inside and talk to me.

Sitting at my kitchen table, the officers told me that they had received an emergency call from Teton County asking them to come to my home and do a welfare check because my car had been found in a ditch totaled and shot five times by a .38 caliber gun.

I said that the car had been parked in the garage with the door closed, and my keys were inside the house, so whoever had stolen and trashed the car must have also broken into my home. I was horrified now, breathing hard.

Apparently the invaders had rolled my 2001 Pontiac Grand Prix right out of our family's electronic garage. With Mark's help, we immediately put in an electronic security system. Motion detectors, hidden microphones, and thermal sensors surrounded us, especially at night. The police never discovered who did it, but the timing and bullet holes were plenty sinister for me. I decided to purchase a gun, a Lady Smith with a rosewood handle.

By 2004, our home had eight computers up and running. Back in 2002, after our original computer crashed while I was using it, Randy had custom-built me my own machine. But now his business had grown along with my work, and expansion was required. Luckily, my husband the hardware genius could build even better machines than what you could buy commercially from Dell or HP. Randy's computers were much cheaper, and you weren't locked into having to buy an entire board. I was thrilled to have so much to work with, and I know Randy was more than happy to have his computer and records far away from me!

I WAS GROWING QUITE SOPHISTICATED in my various undercover roles. I was primarily using the identities of Abu Musa and Abu Zeida, which I had created for roles as a recruiter and trainer, respectively. These two occupations seemed to hold the most allure for the largest number of targets, but if I needed to produce a courier or financier I also had those identities ready to go, already planted in various Internet forums and messages groups.

My first focus has always been threats related to the U.S., or any of our interests abroad, and individuals wishing to harm the U.S. tend to come from every corner of the globe. Of course, I have never ignored information that might cause harm or destruction to any other country in the world. There are those cases that start out looking innocuous, but when you connect the dots to a bigger picture, a threat materializes. Then there are the big talkers that sound so outrageous initially that you might roll your eyes and pass them off as wannabes. The only way to distinguish between those that present potential threats and those that can be ignored is to look closely at every one. One day in April of 2006, I was going through my morning routine of checking the different Yahoo and Orkut message groups for any new postings by individuals I was following. That particular morning I was reading through the messages posted overnight at the "al_neda_cell" group when I came across a new member going by the screen name of "jihadlover@yahoo.com." The al_neda_cell group wasn't conducted exclusively or even primarily in Arabic, but the message posted that morning from jihadlover still rang strange—it was in English and simply said, "where can I buy or locate suicide bomb belt." I thought,

"Huh. Where did this joker come from?" I clicked open the "view source" tab in the message, which functions much like a "view headers" function does in emails. I read down to the originating IP address, copied it down, and typed it into my IP tracing program. I gasped when I saw where it had come from—a Station K of the U.S. State Department in Washington, D.C.! So here was some person sitting in a cubicle at Station K in the State Department trying to find out where he or she could obtain a suicide belt. If I wasn't already familiar with the block of IP addresses associated with government agencies, I might have thought—or hoped—that jihadlover was a master spoofer and able to appear as though he was coming from the State Department as some kind of ruse, but I knew that wasn't likely. I quickly copied all of the message headers, as well as jihadlover's message and Yahoo email ID, and sent them off to Mark, saying that someone needed to get hold of the State Department and find this idiot at Station K and tell them that his message requesting information on suicide belts was unprofessional. In my protectiveness of my message groups and jihadist forums, I didn't want jihadlover posting further messages where anyone could locate his IP address. My jihadist friends would scatter in seconds. I was fairly certain that jihadlover's venture into the al_ neda_cell group was not officially sanctioned, but if it was, that would be even worse. I thought, boy, are we in trouble if the government is that sloppy. Then there are times when individuals come on the jihadist scene who are so prolific, and so desperately seeking attention, that several people begin tracking them and report them to authorities. In my opinion, this has both pros and cons for a given situation. Of course, it's a good thing that people are being vigilant and reporting suspicious activities and behavior. On the other hand, sometimes these other private individuals who aren't knowledgeable about the law and who are not working with the knowledge or permission of authorities such as the FBI can make it harder to rein in an individual and deter-mine the nature or potential threat they might present.

I encountered this situation with an individual using the screen name of "kashmirmujahideen." "KM," as I called him, showed up in early 2005 in several Yahoo message groups. KM posted his "profile" (which contained a picture of a man with a black ski mask cover-ing his face, holding an AK-47) in a message group that I was work-ing in called "Tanthem-alqa3edah." KM came across as one of those emotionally disturbed individuals who had delusions of grandeur. He claimed to be a twenty-one-year-old man who was "living in the USA for now." It didn't take long for me to identify KM as one Justin Kadafi Singleton, who lived in the area of Hartford, Connecticut.

KM came on the scene hard and fast, and appeared to be trying to establish himself as some important radical terrorist, claiming he was with a group called "Tanzeem Qaedat Ansar al-Quran" and af-filiated with al-Qaeda. KM's messages seemed to be copied and pasted from other resources, and he profiled inconsistently, but since he was located in the U.S. and calling himself an al-Qaeda affiliate I contin-ued to compile all of the messages he posted in the various message groups, looking for signs of escalation.

Some of KM's rambling messages displayed his underlying hatred of the U.S. He wrote in broken English, things like, "america Troops occupied Somalia during 1993 and masscre many people every place." Trying to further his claim of ties to al-Qaeda, KM declared in one message:

We [al-Qaeda] declared jihad against the US government, because the US government is unjust, criminal and tyrannical. It has committed acts that are extremely unjust, hideous and criminal whether directly or through its support of the Israeli occupation of the Prophet's Night Travel Land (Palestine). And we believe the US is directly responsible for those who were killed in Palestine,

Lebanon and Iraq.

KM also posted statements stating that the U.S. would be invaded by Muslims from the "mideast and asia will dress like americans and talk, walk, act like americans, america will bring in bible study and Christian priest to make muslims to covent to americans."

KM also attempted to send rallying messages calling for the Sunni and Shia Muslims to unite against the U.S. and Western world, stating that he was "not going sit home and watch the western cowards do it i love allah and islam to much to sit on my sofa im ready for jihad . . . thank you." I finally concluded that KM's messages were cries for help from a person in desperate need of attention. I couldn't imagine any truly dangerous person being realistically influenced by his statements.

My email contact with KM was limited, and I finally stopped following him after reading a message he posted that he wanted to be martyred and come back to life and be martyred again and come back to life again. Almost at the same time, I was alerted to a private blog where an individual who had been trying to "sting" kashmirmujahideen posted all of his email communications with KM and basically disrupted my ability to further probe KM.

The only valuable lesson I took from the KM incident was what flaming jihadist wannabes truly looked like. He would be the standard to measure all others against. I had packaged up my materials on KM and passed him on to the FBI just before I discovered the private blog, and my last inquiry to Mark about it was that I hoped that he didn't really present a threat. Mark advised that he had the attention of the FBI and JTTF out in Connecticut, and it was their baby now.

The flip side of a case like KM, however, is a much scarier place.

One such case involved an individual named Mohammed Radwan Obeid, a thirty-three-year-old Jordanian. Obeid came to the United States on a conditional visa in 2001 after marrying an American woman in his native Jordan. At the time he hit my radar, he was living in Dayton, Ohio.

Obeid came to my attention in one of the Internet forums, using the screen name of "ahmed_assalafil" and email ID of "let_us_reason 2005@yahoo.com," where he had been posting information on how to build an H-bomb and other weapons at home. Obeid claimed to be a university student studying nuclear physics. The few messages we exchanged related to claims he had made in the jihad den about recruiting individuals in other countries to come to the U.S. to carry out a secret plan that would rival 9/11. His IP address traced back to a public library in Dayton. I was concerned enough that I had come across yet another individual sitting in America's heartland, claiming to have an important background in nuclear physics as well as having started the recruiting process for a 9/11-level attack, that I decided he needed to be in the hands of the FBI. I packaged up all of his forum postings as well as the background and profile that I had constructed to that point, and sent my package off to Mark in March of 2005.

I would later learn that I was not the only individual who had been concerned about Obeid's suspicious activities and behavior. He was apparently alarming enough to gain the attention of a few other individuals who also reported him to the FBI. Among them were a local police officer who had grown suspicious of Obeid's behavior, and a librarian at a public library in Troy, Ohio, where he had been looking up bomb-making information on one of the public computers.

Obeid was arrested in March of 2005 on fraud and immigration charges and eventually sentenced to a year in prison for lying to FBI and JTTF investigators about his online activity in the jihadist forums, as well as sending numerous emails to different individuals about support for terrorism. They conducted an official investigation into whether he had provided or attempted to provide material support to terrorists. He was deported back to Jordan in November of 2006.

The government's sentencing memorandum stated that Obeid had aggressively attempted to recruit various individuals via the Internet into his radical Islamic causes and enterprise. The subjects of his efforts spanned the U.S., the Philippines, Kuwait, Jordan, Egypt, and Iraq. It also stated that Obeid had visited and interacted in websites describing how to smuggle mujahideen inside the U.S., how to construct hydrogen bombs, encrypt email messages, construct ultra-secure sixteen-digit computer passwords; and a domestic terrorist plan described as "Operation Oklahoma II."

What I learned from the case of Mohammed Radwan Obeid is that staying vigilant regarding suspicious activities really can pay off. In this case, a handful of people in different areas of the country independently observed an individual engaged in behavior alarming and disturbing enough to report to the authorities. Whether or not Obeid would have acted on his claims we will never know, but that's why it's important to stop those who claim to be threats before they truly become them.

In the summer of 2005, I followed an online jihadist whose email address identified him as "Black Flag." Black Flag showed up in the ekhlaas Internet forum or the Islamic Faithfulness Network, posting that he had an important scientific background in nuclear physics and that he wanted to offer his skills to al-Qaeda to do his Muslim duty for jihad. Of course, he caught my attention right away. At the time I was using my Abu Musa identity in the ekhlaas forum, and decided to privately message him through the forum to start the process of confirming whether he in fact had a background in nuclear physics, which of course would be of great value to al-Qaeda.

Early on it became my practice to get individuals to communicate directly with me by cautioning that posting open messages about important matters drew only the wrong kind of attention to them—possibly even the spies and infidels that could be present and trying to monitor activity within the forums. This tactic had served me well over the years, and this time was no exception.

Abu Musa had been a member of the many variations of the ekhlaas forum over the years. Often, the jihadist forums quickly became popular ground for posting and providing terrorist support materials like documents and manuals on how to train yourself for jihad, propaganda and recruitment information, and even videos depicting beheadings and terrorist attacks and their aftermath. As they grew in popularity, watchdog groups took up a concerted effort to have the sites taken down. The effort, though noble, was almost totally ineffective. Within days or sometimes hours, the sites would pop up on another server elsewhere in the world—so it became a game of whack-a-mole. I found it annoying myself—while I understand the motive, these sites have a serious intelligence value that would not otherwise exist, and disrupting one of the most effective routes to follow the activities and trends of the terrorist groups and their ever-growing support base is not particularly helpful in bringing them to justice. I got frustrated when I was focused on something in a particular forum that became an ongoing case, only to find that the site had been taken down and have to wait for it to reappear somewhere else. When this process began in earnest, I decided that I would always keep one long-term identity active so that I would be notified by the administrators when the site was back up and running, without having to reregister. So the maintenance of these long-term identities was critical to a consistent and credible presence.

Based on the content of Black Flag's posts, I knew that if I didn't get him into my web soon, someone else would. That was always the challenge—trying to be the first to snag someone before he fell prey to another individual who might truly be able to take him down the path he sought.

Black Flag claimed that he had been an associate professor in the field of nuclear physics at a university in the Middle East. By the time I was able to get him talking to me, first through private messaging in the forum, then together by email, he had already begun to post digital pictures of himself with what he claimed were various components and materials needed to construct a hydrogen bomb. When I finally had his word that he would no longer post anything on the Internet about this "important and valuable work," he began explaining to me his background and education and why he wanted to offer his services to al-Qaeda.

Black Flag and I communicated with each other for just over a month before he began to seriously push for a meeting. I began sending Mark all of the pictures, diagrams, and schematics of Black Flag's directions for construction of an H-bomb. Mark instructed me to see if he would take digital pictures of himself showing each step required to construct the bomb.

I was indeed able to convince him, by saying that if he was able to provide me with credible documentation that he had the skills and experience to build this bomb, and if my superiors approved and our "Sheik" agreed to secure the financing for such a project, we would coordinate a meeting with him and potentially invite him into our group. Black Flag was all too eager to proceed with proving his abilities. In our final communications, he asked again about joining my group, as well as where his work would be performed. Having no personal knowledge of hydrogen bombs or a background in nuclear physics, I brought in one of the few trusted individuals I allowed into my Internet work—and the only person in the world I knew that had any ability to determine the viability of Black Flag's H-bomb claims— my nuclear physicist friend up in Canada, the only 7Seas colleague I still spoke to.

I packaged up all of the documents, photos, diagrams, and schematics to send to my colleague for his analysis and determination. He eventually advised me that he believed that what Black Flag had provided to me as substantiation might actually be valid. In light of this, I decided that going any further with Black Flag myself would be irresponsible. Like so many others, my profile of Black Flag was packaged up and sent off to Mark in hopes that all of the information I'd gathered would be properly routed to experts who could take this case further.

CHAPTER TEN

THE 9/11 OF ENERGY

In October of 2005, another anti-U.S. individual appeared one day in the Osama bin Laden—OBL Crew—Yahoo message group, which I was trying to control, posting under the screen name of "longtermonly2@yahoo.com." Longtermonly2 was dropping hints about some important plan in an attempt to get group members interested in him. The OBL Crew was a message group that communicated primarily in Arabic. It was obvious that long termonly2 only spoke English, as he left his messages in broken English. At the time, I wasn't in the mood for this "newbie" who claimed to be an angry American bent on causing some cataclysmic event to screw up our foreign policy, forcing the recall of U.S. military troops home from Afghanistan and Iraq. However, longtermonly2's appearance in the OBL Crew group had shades of Specialist Ryan Anderson, who had come onto my radar in another Yahoo message group just two years earlier. My guard was up. Longtermonly2's first message in the OBL Crew group, posted on October 25, 2005, stated:

it is true america has overstepped its bounds in invading Iraq, those serious

enough to do something about it should email militiapal2@yahoo.com there is a

plan if you only truly seek to commit to it. Contact soon, as a return to USA will

negate emails thru this website. We both want something, lets talk.

A

There were a couple of red flags in his message, especially the fact that he had left a contact email address bearing the name of "militia-pal2," a possible indication of extremist beliefs, which individuals of militia-type groups often harbor. Also, longtermonly2 indicated he was not in the U.S. but was planning to return soon. Back in 2005, Yahoo message groups still allowed you to view the source code of each message, which usually contained the originating IP address for the person posting the message. As is my practice when possible, I traced his IP addresses for anything suspicious or strange, and it led me to a server for Assumption College Thonburi in Bangkok, Thailand. At the time I didn't know what to make of longtermonly2 or his location. So I didn't make contact right away, deciding instead to wait and observe anything else he posted.

Two days later, on October 27, longtermonly2 posted again, only this time his screen name contained the name "Michael Reynolds." Now he had my attention. His first message had indicated he was not in the U.S. but would be returning within a couple of weeks, and I had already determined that whoever "Michael Reynolds" and long-termonly2 actually were, they were located in Thailand and somehow associated with Assumption College in Bangkok. The October 27 message posted at the OBL Crew site read:

Still awaiting someone serious about contact. Only 2 weeks until I return to USA.

Would be a pity to lose this idea. Can make all the difference, but must cotact

me asap.

His tone was serious, indicating his impatience. Again, I decided not to initiate contact with longtermonly2 but to wait and see what his next move might be.

Then, on October 28, in a message titled "reality," longtermonly2 posted:

> OK, posting obvious messages doesn't work apparently function. Lets make it simple. Week and a half left, does anyone actually read this or does it just blog to the waste can? Real oppurtunities dont fall from the sky like is being lost here. If any real member of the OBL crew is reading these, do something besides ignoring them. email me.

Longtermonly2 obviously felt he was sitting on something of importance. This last message began to garner attention from the group. I noticed he had received replies from two members of the group known as soldierfisabilillah@yahoo.com and binabdullah@yahoo.com. Both of these individuals were known to be hard and radical, often posting graphic pictures and videos depicting gore and bloodshed resulting from car bombings and other attacks, which were praised by group members. Seeing the start of interaction between longtermonly2 and these members of the group, I decided that it was time to try to draw him into my lair instead. I activated one of my identities that had been used in the group, "Hani Yousef Alomari," aka "Abu Zeida," which I had been using for over two years at the time.

The biography I had created for Abu Zeida was a colorful one of a bloodthirsty, impatient, radicalized jihadist who claimed affiliation with the Lashkar-e-Tayyiba (LeT), meaning Army of the Righteous. LeT is one of the largest and most active of the mujahideen groups operating mainly out of Pakistan, and was known to have become formally associated with al-Qaeda elements operating in the Af-Pak region. I chose LeT for Abu Zeida because it would be hard for any of the individuals I communicated with in the jihadi sites to disprove who Abu Zeida was or his involvement with any of the terrorist attacks claimed or attributed to LeT. To bolster Abu Zeida's jihadist prowess, I had researched the facts behind several LeT attacks, seeking those that were abstract enough yet still on record for Abu Zeida to have participated in. For instance, I chose a drive-by shooting targeting a U.S. consulate that killed five and injured thirteen back in January of 2002, and a grenade attack against a Christian church in Pakistan that left four dead, including two U.S. citizens, and forty-six injured in March of 2002. Though Abu Zeida had an honorable mujahideen background, I had mobilized him from an "active operative" conducting attacks with LeT into the role of a recruiter and trainer.

Before I actually made my first contact with longtermonly2, I pieced together all of the information I had obtained relating to his longtermonly2 and militiapal2 email addresses, as well as the name Michael Reynolds and Assumption College. It was a sketchy start, but that's pretty standard in such cases until the lines of communication are open and flowing.

On November 3, 2005, Abu Zeida's first contact with Reynolds was to simply inquire about his plan. It said:

> please let me know what plan is about if we can help with you email ok and be
> careful

Reynolds replied back to me that same day advising that his great "plan" was:

> the plan is about recall of foreign troops home as well as firing of their boss,
> making further troubles from them impossible, more data will be provided, at
> length upon contracting services, interested? I found the key.

His message was almost as vague as the previous ones, but did provide a bit more detail. I thought his last comment, that he had "found the key," was a bit cryptic. At this point I decided to create a dossier of what I had and send it off to Mark. By all indications, Michael Reynolds was a U.S. citizen who was presently in Thailand and would return home to the U.S. soon. This was certainly going to be the jurisdiction of the FBI if it became an actual case or investigation.

The next morning, November 4, I compiled my materials and sent them off by email to Mark, explaining that because this individual was reaching out to al-Qaeda to assist him with his "plan" and his tone indicated urgency and impatience, I wanted to talk to Mark as soon as possible so I didn't lose my line with Reynolds.

I continued watching the OBL Crew for any other messages from Reynolds or indication that he was communicating with others in the group. Initially, Mark said that the information and details I had provided were interesting but he wasn't convinced Reynolds presented any viable threat or indication he might become one. So I was free to continue communicating with Reynolds, prodding him deeper about the details of his "plan" to see if he was just a big talker or if he indeed intended something dastardly.

I didn't see anything posted by Reynolds on the OBL Crew site or receive any other messages from him until November 13 when he emailed Abu Zeida asking:

are your people seriously considering this opportunity, its time to decide, if so we need a meeting and discussion on cash availability. With recent press, this is the ideal time.

Mike.

I waited until later that day to reply to his email, and I decided to play it cool and as generic as possible while also indicating that "my

group" was interested, and that in order to provide any financial assistance I would need more details. I was in my fishing phase with him
now, and I had to proceed with as much caution as possible while still
dangling enough good bait to keep him interested. I also decided that
it was time to employ my signature hook—telling him to set up an
email account and send me the password and we would communicate
in the draft folder. My November 13 email to Reynolds stated:

> we can be redy withyou . . for money asistance tell me what is plan and what
>
> you need from us and it be good idea if you set up new email and we give
>
> messiges with each other in draft file so we donttalk important matter over
>
> internet you send me email account and password and we talk there

Within one hour, Reynolds had dutifully complied with my request and sent me an email from the new account he had created. The
new email account he had set up was called homeapproach@yahoo
.com, and he was now going by the name of "Fritz Mueller." Reynolds's message to me from the new email account stated:

> this is your new email contact for me that you asked for. what ill need is some
>
> travelling cash, to observe what we seek, and help in Texas, Alaska, and 2 units
>
> in Ny area. what can you do quickly? I think it best to only pass info on each
>
> step to each section head, for everyones security.
>
> Fritz

I took the fact that he created the new email account with the
name of "homeapproach" as an indicator that he was serious about
his claim of returning to the U.S. Later that night, as I deciphered
the email headers associated with this new account, I discovered
that the IP address led to an Internet provider located in Wilkes-

Barre, Pennsylvania. Apparently, sometime between November 6 and 13, Reynolds had indeed traveled home to the U.S. One theme Reynolds had been pressing since he first popped up at the OBL Crew group was that he was in need of financial assistance, which he continued to reiterate. However, the details of his "plan" were now also starting to surface. He had provided locations within the U.S., and clearly had something of a strategy in mind, but it would take careful digging on my part to pull those details out of him. He was definitely providing snippets as the tiny bread crumbs that would lead me to discover what he had in mind. How serious he was, I had still not determined.

I packaged up this latest round of emails from Reynolds to forward on to Mark for his review and guidance. As expected, though, it was still not enough to make much of a determination as to what this guy's plan actually entailed. That was fine with me, as I relish the challenge of ferreting out information from people, and Reynolds was definitely my most fascinating new project.

As the case proceeded, I continued to research and obtain background history and information on Michael Curtis Reynolds to update my profile and threat assessment. He had a checkered past that included not only criminal activity, but a dishonorable discharge from the Army and financial difficulties resulting in tax liens. He was born in Mount Kisco, New York, and graduated from North Salem High School, also in Westchester County, in 1976. In 1978, he was convicted of trying to blow up his family's Purdys, New York, home, but given a conditional discharge after pleading guilty to a misdemeanor charge of fourth-degree attempted arson. His criminal history also included arrests and convictions for disorderly conduct and breach of the peace. He was also named on legal documents related to tax liens against him and to outstanding debts.

In the early 1980s he married Tammy Danise, and the couple had three children but later divorced. Reynolds spent time as a member of a radical state militia in the early 1980s. He had been trained in karate and the martial arts, reaching the level of black belt. He also had training in the use of explosives and firearms.

The profile I was developing indicated that Reynolds had the potential to present a viable and escalating threat not only to himself but to society.

Reynolds's message the next day, November 14, was titled "plan" and revealed further details:

> since tracing is an issue, I plan each section to make only one communications
>
> run, ill do NYC units, Texas will meet me in Florida, Alaska will travel to Texas.
>
> This will make finding patterns of travel prior to activity hard if not impossible.
>
> Instructions will pass from the traveller to the units, eliminating mail traces as
>
> well. Im trying to make security for all. Is the issue of payment for this something
>
> we need to discuss now, or in steps as its done?
>
> Fritz

My fears of a repeat of the Anderson case were starting to rise. Not only were Anderson and Reynolds both U.S. citizens and located in the U.S., but both had wanted something from al-Qaeda or to offer something to the terrorist group. Whereas Anderson had wanted to defect from the Army and join al-Qaeda, Reynolds was attempting to partner up or co-opt the services of al-Qaeda as a part of his plan. But there was one obvious difference. At the time I came into contact with Ryan Anderson in 2003, he was trying to contact al-Qaeda to defect from the Army prior to deploying to Iraq. Anderson didn't have a plan for how to defect or what he could offer to al-Qaeda initially; that came much later. I was only two weeks into communicating and interacting with Reynolds, and I could see that he was more methodical and calculating, having formulated his plan even before he popped up in the OBL Crew group. Reynolds was way ahead of the game. And he wanted cash quickly.

By this time, I wondered if his "plan" was just a ruse to manipulate me into providing him financial assistance and then disappear. I had to laugh at this thought, thinking that if Reynolds truly believed he was in fact collaborating with an al-Qaeda operative, he had to have some idea of the trouble he would be in if he were to take the money and run! I was also weighing his past and criminal history, which were admittedly troubling, against the likelihood that he in fact intended to set in motion a plan that would be categorized as a terrorist activity—a much larger crime than any of his previous infractions. There were a lot of unknowns that needed to be figured out before any viable threat assessment could be finalized.

Within a few hours of sending me his "plan" email, another message arrived in Abu Zeida's in-box, titled "timing," wherein he added:

would like to start this project soon, seems everything is in our favor, but might

not last long. please let me know what we can do about travel funds, and

contact info, starting with NY.

Again, he was pressing for cash without saying exactly what his plan was.

I didn't take long to decide how I would respond to this latest lack of revelation. I wanted to give him the impression that, as a seasoned al-Qaeda recruiter, I could reach into my "contacts bag" and activate people to help with his plan, within a believable proximity, though not too close, to the locations he had mentioned in his previous emails. Though I had already concluded that Reynolds was ahead of me in strategy, it was important that I give him some comfort and reassurance that I had an ability to accommodate him as we went forward. Once I was comfortable in the areas I had selected to propose in response to his latest revelations, I sent off my reply:

> Hello my firend, i rang some contacts with my group in usa today. . i have 1 person in ny and 1 in pensilvania . we can have more involved and I can arrang some $ if i can tell ny guy what he is to do with this . florida I have person in georgia who is close to florida can help to . we can talk of detail here in email and no telefone or mobile telefone to talk of our plans . . . i suggest that you make details in a document and attach to email so it is not intercepted . . we have use this process and its safe . . you may call me Hani, my name

Within an hour Reynolds confirmed what I already knew from tracing his IP address—that he was here in the U.S. and located in Wilkes-Barre. His reply read:

> ok Hani, Im in Pa, near wilkes barre. is that close?

The next day, November 15, he sent another nudge for funds, saying:

> Im hoping no one is offended that I require payment for this service, but as I said, ill have to leave permanently, and ill need to not set up a permanent residence while this is forming, that requires funds to do. Any chance that there is an Id passport program you can hook me up with?
> Fritz

I thought, even if I had access to money to send him, he couldn't realistically expect that this would happen or that he had presented enough details of his fantastical "plan" to encourage me to do so! His email that day was titled "offended." I thought, he sure demands a lot while providing very little!

I didn't respond to Reynolds's November 15 email, as I had sent off my updated profile and threat assessment to Mark and was waiting to find out how much further I should go with my investigation. If the FBI wasn't going to enter into the picture soon, I was going to have to develop an exit strategy, because the thing Reynolds wanted and needed the most was money, and if I didn't give it to him he would soon take his request elsewhere.

Several days passed and I hadn't observed any activity in the OBL Crew group involving Reynolds or received any further email messages. Then, on November 21, Reynolds sent off an email titled "needs" to Abu Zeida that stated:

> can we agree this week on a down payment to cover travel costs, and a final
> total payment? I hate to rush, but next week could ruin schedules.
> Fritz

Reynolds had sent his latest email from his "longtermonly2" email account, abandoning the "homeapproach" account. I wasn't sure if this was significant. In tracing the IP addresses in the headers of his latest email, I confirmed he was no longer in Pennsylvania. His IP address now traced to the Pocatello, Idaho, area. He had been on the move, apparently across the country, which would explain his absence over the last several days. I couldn't come up with any reason why he went to Idaho. The locations for the targets he had selected for his "plan" did not correspond geographically with his present location. I was uneasy knowing that he was now closer than comfort to me. I even considered the idea that maybe the jig was up on me and that he was aware that I was not Abu Zeida. Or, God forbid, that he was al-Qaeda and was on his way to find me.

I called Mark that morning after I had got to work and told him that Reynolds had traveled from Pennsylvania to the Pocatello, Idaho, area but that I had no idea or explanation for why he was there. I mentioned my feelings about his proximity to me and the general unsettled nature of the case.

At lunch I went back through the email headers for every email I had sent to Reynolds, making sure that there were no missing "hops" in the Internet packets from the proxy IP address I was using—hops measure the delays or problems in transit across an Internet Protocol (IP) network. All of my tracks appeared to have been disguised. Maybe I was just being paranoid. I couldn't think of any other reason Reynolds would suspect I was not who I said I was.

It was now three days before Thanksgiving, and I knew that Mark and his family would be away for the holiday. I had been working to keep Reynolds on the hook and talking, but I was concerned that if I didn't respond to him before the holiday I would lose him. I was pressing Mark for a decision. Mark advised that the FBI really needed more details from Reynolds about his plan and what his intentions were, and that if we could get this information before Thanksgiving a decision could be made. I was going to have to carefully step up the pressure on Reynolds without violating evidentiary rules or his constitutional rights. Tricky.

On November 23, the day before Thanksgiving, I replied to Reynolds, instructing him as follows:

fritz, interest in the holiday plan is good and i aware the time is short and

delivery may take much time. We move it fast if all is ok . I need to know more for the item we purchase. We have resource but not wiling to commit resource without further detail. Follow this instructions by detail and no more contact at this e-mail address [xxxxxxxxxxxxx] from this message.

> Today you do this
>
> > - you go to hotmail.com
> >
> > - sign in account abu_qtada777@hotmail–p/w [xxxxxx]
> >
> > - point to and click Mail
> >
> > - point to and click Draft
> >
> > - open message in this Draft folder i call description of holiday item
> >
> > - type description regardig item you describe in detail for our purchase. Do not leave detail unreported
> >
> > - point to and click Save Draft
> >
> > - sign out and do not point to and click Send–if you point to and click send i will not respond
> >
> > - do not go in this account again until one whole day gone- then do same as
>
> I write above to look at new drafte message for instruction about payment if item you tell me meets our needs

Again, within an hour, Reynolds replied to my instructions with an email message written in coded speech, meaning it was up to me to read between the lines. His message read:

Theres little time, due to how busy we all get during the holidays. Theres much shopping to do, travel to plan, rental cars, not to mention all the presents to wrap. What I need is to have my Christmas bonus, plus the total budget plan so I don't disappoint anyone, especially myself with how much I have to work with. If youre truly serious about this, I wont release the secret santa list until I have the bonus. We have only 3 weeks of shopping and planning left. I have travel to do before then and meet the family members, give out the list of charities to receive the gifts, and help them shop. You need to decide if you want the

presents, otherwise I might have to locate another charity, which would ruin the

holidays for all of us. I thought that you wanted the Christmas gifts that I had for

you, do you?

Fritz

Reynolds had attached a document to this email titled "Theres little time" that contained more details of his plan. I also checked the abu-qtada email account to see if he had left anything in the draft folder as I had instructed. He had. He also left the contents of his "Theres little time" attachment in the body of the message saved in the draft folder. It read:

if I give too many details, theres no need to hire me, yet you want proof of

the reality. Ok, not full details, but enough. The key is 3 parts. The first was

learned from Katrina, it was fuel. When the storm took out production for only

2 days, doubled the cost of gas, and the government did nothing to stop it.

The people here are truly pissed about it. We recreat tht on a bigger scale,

taking out production for weeks, maybe more. Multiple sites, compounds the

problem of rerouting the fuel to solve it. Take out the only backup plan, namely

Alaska Pipeline, do it in a way to get the enviromentalists involved, the govt,

the enviromentalists, and the gas users will be at each others throats. Now top

that with a reason to recall the national guard not only to safeguard this in the

future, but its peiople, making NYC get a black eye for all its new security on

the subways just to be foiled. The americans will trample Washington to recall

troops, if it isnt quick enough, use the press to make people believ the govt

not only knew about this, but allowed this in an effort to continue the war, the

people will make a new govt for you. It will reinforce the idea that some have

about continued if not larger retributions since invasion. This is whata missing

in 4 years, nothing has been done since, so it appears that the govt was right to invade, making retailiations cease. thats the opinion people have, true or not.

Use that. Thats the plan. it needs 1 bus, 4 propane trucks, several additional

items, all to be seperated until used to dispell discovery. is that enough

information? I cannot announce destinations as yet without some proof from

you, whats it to be? want more? . .agree on an amount.

Fritz

The only words I could muster after reading Reynolds's message were "Oh, dear God." I sat there staring at the computer screen and made myself reread his message a couple more times as I tried to process everything. Reynolds wanted to blow up the Trans-Alaska Pipeline, disrupting production and the flow of crude oil through the pipeline for weeks, hopefully forcing the government to recall U.S. troops from abroad. This time, his request was straightforward: he wanted one bus and four propane trucks. My guess was that he intended to place the bus and propane trucks at strategic points along the pipeline. Clearly, Reynolds was farther along with his plan than I had ever imagined. Now, he said that if I wanted more information about locations for his targets, he would need to be paid for his services.

Yet I still had nothing but his words. Finding outside confirmation that he in fact intended to blow up the pipeline would be my next priority and objective.

Knowing that time was of the essence, I called Mark immediately and said, "Reynolds's plan is to blow up the Alaska Pipeline, and he is going to do it with a bus likely loaded with explosives and the strategic placement of four propane trucks along the pipeline. He also said that if I want more details about the locations of his other targets, we needed to agree on an amount for his services." There was dead silence on the other end of the line. I said, "Mark, are you there? Did you hear what I just said?" He replied, "Yes, and I am very concerned by the fact he is now in Idaho just a couple hundred miles away and that at the very least, whether he has the means available to him to actually carry out an attack on the pipeline or not, he has definitely proffered a threat against critical infrastructure." He advised me to wait as long as I could to reply, because he was going to have to make some calls and see where we should take this from here. Before he hung up, Mark said, "You better not ruin my Thanksgiving!" The joke was a welcome moment of relief. That afternoon, things had definitely jumped to a new level.

The next day, November 24, I checked the abu_qtada email account to see if Reynolds had left any new messages in the draft folder. He had. Reynolds was revealing his intent through his words, and I was pretty certain he wasn't aware how critically important this was to any possible criminal prosecution.

> I wanted to pass details one by one to eliminate anyone getting the entire
> plan, but I can give you guidelines. Plan is to force recall of home support
> units from abroad, by making no place safe, cutting gas supplies to raise cost
> astronomically, forcing people to fight government, playing the press against the
> govt, letting slip the govt knew and did nothing. That's the outline, so as far as
> cash, whats it worth to complete? Ill have to relocate away after this, as I wont
> be popular, know what I mean? I can give missions abroad in the future, but
> want to see how business goes this time. We need an amount that we both can
> live with.

Reynolds's words indicated that he believed his plan would affect U.S. foreign policy as well as dramatically impact our energy infrastructure. What Reynolds was essentially proposing was the 9/11 of Energy Infrastructure. If Reynolds was successful in carrying out his plan, he could conceivably achieve his desired results. However, there was no way Mark and I were going to let that happen.

The day after Thanksgiving, Mark called me and said that he had been able to coordinate with the FBI's Pocatello field office in Idaho and that the FBI would be taking over the case. He also told me to go ahead and prepare one last message for Reynolds and to send it to him to review before I left it in the draft folder.

I sat at my desk trying to think of what to say that might buy time for the FBI. I had brought in a load of laundry that I was folding while thinking.

One of my tactics that I use when communicating with my targets is trying to create a level of mystery and intrigue regarding who my identities are. Sometimes I will create a new identity for the purpose of diversion. Since I was going to be buying time in this case, diversion through the introduction of a new member of my group as a new contact for Reynolds was in order. As I pondered the possible name of a new "contact" for Reynolds, I had one of my daughter's shirts in my hands, inside out, so the label was visible. The name on the label was "Massimo." For some reason I liked it, though it wasn't an Arab name. I remember thinking, "Does that really matter, though? He believes I have contacts in the U.S., and it might make for a little twist or diversion for him to think that his contact wouldn't be of Arab heritage." I figured that would make things more comfortable, in case when it came time to meet in person he would be meeting a contact of Italian descent, which would make more sense in Idaho than someone who looked like an Arab. I decided to name Reynolds's contact "Messimo," which sounded more like a male name than "Massimo." Anyway, if Mark didn't like it, I had plenty of Arab names I could change it to.

I wanted to make sure that I addressed as many of the outstanding details that Reynolds had requested as possible, such as funding and obtaining a new ID and passport. I also wanted to provide him with some assurance that my group had contacts in the Alberta, Canada, area that could be easily mobilized to Alaska for the operation.

I put together what I thought was a clever and comprehensive message for Mark to review and sent it off. We talked over the phone about the details of it, and he asked why I chose to say this or that. In fact, the first thing he asked was how I had come up with the name Messimo, and when I explained it he had a good laugh, saying, "Only you, Shannen . . . only you would come up with something like that." I explained my reasoning for choosing a non-Arab name, and he agreed that was probably a good idea. In the end, only a few things were changed. The final version of the message left in the draft folder said:

messimo is supereor for our group and is one who give us $ for this. he wants to talk with you and give both some trust of each other befour I travel to usa . he very much like this idea and goal of it and if it is sucessful his interest will benefit. there is a commiting to operation now and we get 1/2 of amount for transfer and if he is satisfid with plan he give out rest of $. messimo will make sure all of amount is in a usa depository so $ can to get out quick for operation. I travel to usa and I come with partner and he is jaouad. he knows englaish and went to university in usa. so we need amount for $ and how we set the transfering for this. there is also need to know if you want purchasing or the rent for bus and trucks this makes differance for amount for $ or if you have these now . can you get us this informaition by the coming week ?

messimo want the knowlege if you there is other group working with this and he must know them so no one else can claim this . . . this impourtant for sucess and how we work in europe and middle east . he can have none of lose ends to lead back to group . he will speek to this with you he says. now we have 3 peopel in edmonton, canada and this is close to alaska he will comit them to operation . at the timing for operaton to carry out the us peopel will be disapearing . we have a courier who gives new ID documints . most operatons we have done in europe and middle east but have work in usa befour.

Reynolds did not leave a reply in the draft folder that night or the next day, which was out of step with his pattern of rapidly replying to my messages. On the evening of November 27, Mark and I drafted another message for Reynolds, which said:

our leader is the sheik is very much in liking this operaton idea and goal of it and if this sucesful he has interests to benefit him . i wait for your mesagge the last days and I felt happy to see it tonight. we now talk of your mesagge tonight with the sheik knows the fast time you ask for the $ for operaton and he need to have the knowlege to prepare and for this plan he talks of there a big amount needed. there is need to know if there is need for purchasing or for the rent of bus and trucks this makes differance for amount for $ or if you have these now . you have not told me the amount for $ yet and this i waited for to give to group. We very much want this sucess of operaton and to take credit in the name of our sheik and group. the sheik ask to know if there are other group working for you for operaton . for us the small amount of peopel with knowlege of plan help us all for when operaton is completed. we have 3 peopel in edmonton, canada and this is close to alaska who we can send for a comitting to operaton to speed this and allow for us to agree upon a worthy reward . tell me now in next mesagge of cost for plan and then and how we set the transfering of $ for this. you get to me this informaition in the coming days and we move fast and careful for this

The premise of this message was to keep Reynolds intrigued, as well as to give him the idea that things were organized, though complicated. We were also ready to provide him with the amount of money that he believed would be required for his services. The negotiation was under way, but Reynolds was bargaining for more than he ever imagined.

The next day, November 28, Reynolds left a reply to my previous two messages in the draft folder that read:

smaller the better. I have no vehicles, but if we rent them, they will be traceable, be careful. I work alone, as trust is an issue here. So if we cannot borrow the vehicles, we need a way to rent them anonomously, then fill them. I have to travel, so I need funds, Im thinking 10,000usd, plus I would like funds for myself to keep from traceable income from the government. I would value the reward for this in the 100,000+ range, and would like at least 30%, at which time I can do the trips, get the maps, and give full details. in the meantime, we have to shop for all the road flares we can get, no more than 2 packs from any one place. I want no notice taken of our shopping, hope you understand this. Well need 20lb propane cylinders full, and fuse cord. all is easily obtained, minus the truck issues, about 5,000usd I would think. I have since located further irems for us next year. The goal is to so confuse, that resources spent there must be used here. Thats my thinking. if the cash is alright, we must move this week to get me travelling. the others can shop while I research, but I have to quit my job, so I need the funds upfront. 30% is typical for this work, I hope you dont find that or the amount excessive. let me know. it might be possible to borrow trucks nearby where they are needed instead of rentals. I wont know til I travel to see. we need details and maps to make it work. contact me asap. Let the sheik know my missions have never failed, I have done this in other countries for over 24yrs. Fritz

He was asking for roughly forty thousand dollars for his services and had provided more details of his plan than before, indicating that he intended to go forward. In his own words, once he had the money in hand he could shop for the materials required for the operation.

When Reynolds had initially revealed the details of his plan, his first target was the Trans-Alaska Pipeline. Though I was not aware of

it at the time, apparently while he was in the Pocatello area, he had
traveled to the Williams Natural Gas Refinery in Opal, Wyoming, one
of the three biggest natural gas plants in the United States. After cas-
ing the Williams refinery twice, Reynolds concluded that the security
was lax and that access to the facility could be obtained easily. The
quickest and easiest way to attack the refinery would be to blow up
the gas wellheads. Because he was currently closer to the Williams
refinery, an attack could be carried out sooner and more easily than a
strategic attack on the Alaska Pipeline. The Williams refinery became
Reynolds's first target in his plan to take down the U.S. government
and its critical energy infrastructure.

He knew exactly how he wanted to accomplish the attacks, and
promised to lay out the details of his updated plan once he received
the funds he had requested for his services. We settled on the amount
of forty thousand dollars.

Reynolds suggested that the funds be left in a red sack under a
picnic table in a rest area along Interstate 15, just north of Pocatello,
at mile marker one hundred in an area known as Hell's Half Acre.
At first, Reynolds had asked to have the money wired to one of his
accounts, but I told him that was not possible for my group to do.
On December 5, 2005, just after noon, Michael Curtis Reynolds left
Room 205 of the Thunderbird Hotel in Pocatello to drive to the rest
area along I-15 to pick up the forty thousand dollars that al-Qaeda
had promised to leave for him.

Reynolds arrived at the rest area and walked across the crunchy
snow to the designated picnic table, where FBI agents had placed a
red bag containing the money. As soon as the six foot three Reynolds
had the red bag in hand, he took a quick look around, only to find an
FBI SWAT team closing in on him. Reynolds was apprehended by the
SWAT team, forced onto his stomach, and handcuffed.

Just like the coward that he was, in a pathetic attempt to explain his actions that day, he told the FBI agents on the way to the Pocatello FBI office, "You're arresting the wrong guy. I was the one trying to entrap that al-Qaeda person. I was enticing them."

"That story makes no sense," an FBI agent said.

We would soon see that everything Michael Reynolds said from the day he was arrested to the day he was convicted entirely controverted his claim to be conducting an undercover operation as a private mercenary to catch an al-Qaeda cell here in the U.S.

On October 4, 2006, Reynolds would be charged, by superseding indictment by a federal grand jury for the Middle District of Pennsylvania, with four counts of attempting to provide material support and resources to a foreign terrorist organization and two counts of possession of an explosive device. His trial would be held almost two years later.

CHAPTER ELEVEN

MY LAST TESTIMONY

By the end of 2005, my position as a judge for the city of Conrad was on the chopping block, with the possibility that the municipal court would be consolidated with the county's justice court. I had spent over six years on the bench, and though I enjoyed being a judge, I couldn't risk being unemployed in the near future. When they established a commission to study the cost overruns for potential duplication of court services between the city's court and the county's justice court, I had decided to begin looking for other employment. After several months applying for positions in the legal field around the state, I was eventually offered a position with the state's attorney general's office in the field of civil litigation and investigation. I accepted the position in August of 2006, which meant that I would be required to relocate to Helena, the state capital, to live during the week, and would return home to my family in Conrad on the weekends. The situation was not ideal, but considering the slim employment prospects in the legal profession in Montana, I was lucky to have found the job.

The move to Helena was difficult, but it was a sacrifice I had to make in order for my family to survive. It took a couple of months before I got used to the routine of being away from my family during the week, but I loved my job and all the challenges it presented. I have always loved to do legal research and writing, and all facets of litigation. So I spent fifty hours a week consumed with my work, which did help pass the time.

I would spend almost three years at the attorney general's office before I resigned my position in June of 2009 as a result of deteriorating health.

I HAD TAKEN THE JOB with the attorney general's office just two months before Michael Reynolds was indicted on terrorism-related charges in October of 2006. With the grand jury's indictment, I was on course to be a witness in another high-profile terrorism case. The Reynolds trial was set to begin on July 9, 2007, in Scranton, Pennsylvania. I continued to hope that Reynolds would come to his senses and opt for a plea bargain rather than proceed to trial. I harbored this hope for selfish personal reasons, but after having the Anderson case so drastically impact and change my life I was not looking forward to another round. At least this time Mark would be there for the trial and help me see it through.

As the months leading up to trial progressed, we did witness prep through videoconferencing at the U.S. attorney's office in Helena, which I was grateful for, as I didn't want to travel cross-country. And having survived the Anderson case—where it seemed that for me personally anything that could go wrong did go wrong—I felt that I would be a better prepared and adjusted witness this time around.

I worked well over sixty hours the week before I left. Though it was a holiday, I worked through the morning of July 4 to tie up as many loose ends as I could because I didn't know how long I might be stuck in Pennsylvania. I had been feeling very tired and fatigued before I left and was having trouble eating, but I pushed myself to meet my obligations so that nothing would fall on the shoulders of anyone else. The night of the Fourth of July, while I was packing, I became dizzy. I thought I might be coming down with a nasty cold or maybe the flu, and was frustrated because being sick was the very last thing I needed. I lay down on the couch, where I slept for several hours.

The next morning, I left Helena for Scranton, Pennsylvania. Traveling from Montana to almost anywhere requires several stops, since there are no direct flights except to Seattle, Salt Lake City, and Denver. To get to the East Coast can require as few as three stops and as many as five, meaning most of a day. In the case of traveling to Scranton, I made four stops. I arrived around 8:00 that evening and took a taxi to my hotel.

Mark had arrived on July 2. When I was finally settled into my hotel room, I called to let him know I had made it safe and sound. He said to sleep in and rest the next morning as he didn't think the U.S. attorney, John Gurganas, would need to meet with me until the next afternoon. I relished the thought of taking it easy, since I still wasn't feeling on top of things.

The next morning, I woke early and lay in bed until my breakfast arrived. I ordered light food, since I still felt as though I might throw up. I found myself craving milk, and it felt good on my burning stomach, so that I was able to eat some scrambled eggs and toast. After eating my little breakfast, I fell back asleep until close to 11:00, when I woke up startled. I let Mark know that I would walk across to the federal courthouse to meet him after 1:00, and he said that should work out fine.

I left in plenty of time. I was trying not to be nervous at meeting U.S. Attorney John Gurganas for the first time. Though I had talked and videoconferenced with him over the months leading up to the trial, for some reason fears that a latent Major Jenks might surface rumbled inside me.

But Gurganas, a trim, clean-cut man who I guessed to be in his late forties, was friendly, with an ease about him that relaxed me as we went through the case and my witness prep. One of the things that worried me was the fact that Reynolds had received permission from the court to represent himself during the trial, and I was very uneasy about being questioned and cross-examined by him directly. When a defendant is allowed to represent himself, a court will typically assign standby counsel to jump in on the defendant's behalf should their assistance be required, so that proceedings don't have to be delayed to bring in an outside attorney. Reynolds had been assigned local defense attorney Joseph O'Brien as his standby counsel.

Because of this, my witness prep for the Reynolds case differed from that of the Anderson case. Reynolds had been obnoxious and disruptive during pretrial proceedings and was expected to be a loose cannon during the trial. Additionally, Reynolds's six foot three physical stature was imposing and intimidating. In order to make me a stronger witness, Gurganas spent many hours preparing me for insults and accusations, even though it would be the court's job to keep Reynolds in check as much as possible.

Prior to the court appointing O'Brien as Reynolds's standby counsel, he had gone through five defense attorneys, all excused from representing him. Additionally, even when represented by various attorneys, Reynolds fired off handwritten motions for different things, which can happen when defendants are left with a legal tablet, a pen, and time on their hands. Reynolds had filed several lawsuits for things such as writs of habeas corpus, as well as suits against presiding judges and the U.S. attorney's office. All of the claims were ultimately dismissed, but his zeal was unchanged. There was no reason to expect Reynolds would refrain from his usual disruptive and disrespectful behavior in court during the trial.

It is always hard to prepare for the unknown, so it's best to anticipate the worst and hope for the best. In this case, preparing me for almost anything required a lot of time in the remaining two and a half days before trial. We assumed Reynolds would continue in his claim that he had been acting as a mercenary working to uncover al-Qaeda cells here in the U.S., and at all times believed me to be a real al-Qaeda operative whose group he was trying to expose over the Internet in the same manner that I was trying to expose him. It was on this basis that Reynolds would premise a defense, explaining and excusing his actions regarding his plan to carry out attacks on the oil industry to disrupt the government, provoke opposition to the war in Iraq, drive up fuel prices, and help al-Qaeda to terrorize the United States. The reason Reynolds had acted alone and had not sought to alert the authorities about his alleged undercover work to expose terrorists on the Internet was simply because he didn't trust law enforcement.

This meant Reynolds could take his questioning of me as a witness in any number of directions. We used what we already knew about him, and the colorful claims he had made since being arrested back in December of 2005, to make our best guesses. I knew the case best, and I was comfortable with the profile and threat assessment I had compiled of him. I had spent a lot of time in the recent weeks reviewing the materials.

When we finished preparation for my testimony that first day in Scranton, I was feeling calmer. I still wished Reynolds weren't acting as his own attorney for trial. I had seen cases become circuses under

such circumstances. But I was in the hands of competent professionals whose skill and abilities, I believed, coupled with my own, would
allow us to prevail.

Mentally and emotionally, I was leaps and bounds better than I'd
been at Fort Lewis during the Anderson case, when I was a nervous
wreck. Physically, though, the fatigue and nausea I had started to experience before I left Montana was nagging at me. I was not eating
much of anything. I had kept my breakfast down but only felt able to
nibble on a few things the rest of that day. That night I attempted a
bowl of French onion soup but couldn't will myself to finish it.

I was tired, though, and sleep came early that night. I had made
a quick call home to Randy and the kids, but as usual, the kids
weren't home when I called and were out enjoying the summer
night, swimming at the pool or, in the case of my oldest son, practicing with his band for the Battle of the Bands competition at the
end of July. Randy could tell by the sound of my voice that I was
tired, but I didn't bother to worry him about the fact that I wasn't
feeling well. He had vicariously lived through the Anderson case
with me, and though it was hard on me, it had also been hard on
him. I was trying to be strong and not let anything wear me down
this time around.

I slept easily that night, but the next morning I couldn't shake the
fatigue. I decided not to dwell on things and just get ready for the day.
The fact that I was able to eat at all made me think perhaps I was getting over a lingering flu.

It was July 7, two days before trial. Everyone was settled and organized, and the run-through direct examination with Gurganus went
well. We learned later that afternoon that Reynolds would not be representing himself after all; Joseph O'Brien would be taking the helm.
Everyone in the conference room was happy to hear that. I was more

relieved than I let on, but I wanted to appear strong; I wanted them to have faith in me. We decided to do one last run-through with my testimony, in which I was able to tick off the case and how things progressed easily.

Before I left that night, Gurganus explained that he wasn't going to put me on the stand first, and I might not be called until the afternoon on Monday. We decided that to keep the media at bay, I would remain at my hotel until Mark called and the FBI would send a car to pick me up. I felt as though I was finally protected, and I had Mark to thank for that. Gurganus said that if they felt they needed to go over anything with me the next day, he or someone would call, but otherwise I should just take the day and relax.

Leaving the courthouse that day, I actually caught myself smiling, feeling like things might be okay with this trial. I felt that Gurganus and his staff respected me. I also felt like I really had done the right thing. I had not legally or factually entrapped Reynolds. Gurganus had even pointed that out in a few of the email communications I had with Reynolds, which made me feel vindicated. I didn't walk away from the Anderson case feeling that way, but maybe I could this time.

On Sunday, July 8, the day before the trial was set to begin, I took time for myself. Scranton has a strong industrial history in areas of iron and coal mining and railroads. One of the big attractions in Scranton is the Steamtown Train Museum, which wasn't far from my hotel. I found it really interesting. I had loved the eighties song "Allentown" by Billy Joel, named for the Pennsylvania steel town that lay just seventy-five miles to the south of Scranton, and as I explored Scranton that day, I found the song ringing in my head. I wished Randy were there, as I knew that he would have enjoyed the train museum, but I made some mental notes of the details of the exhibits to relay to him later.

Though I had my cell phone with me, the only call I received that day was from Randy. I was glad to not get a call to come back to the courthouse for more witness preparation; I felt ready. I wanted to get the Reynolds case behind me. Randy said that he wasn't crazy about my exploring the city on my own, but I assured him that I was staying very close to the hotel. Besides, since I didn't have a rental car on this trip, I was pretty much left to explore only places within reasonable walking distance of my lodging.

Later that afternoon, I walked toward the downtown area. I was told that Scranton had a sizeable Irish population. Summoning my Irish pride, I decided to check out some of the local pubs. I found a place called Dooley's Pub where I decided to have a simple dinner and ordered the Dublin Burger, which would satisfy me for the night. I was really more interested in the atmosphere than in the menu. I was back in my hotel by 7:30, early enough to get myself relaxed and mentally ready for the next day.

I remember falling asleep early that night, before 10:00. I woke up just after 1:30 a.m. with stomach pain and nausea. I had the last of a bottle of Maalox with me, and I swigged it, hoping that would take care of it. But I couldn't fall back asleep for what seemed like the longest time. I finally woke up after 8:00 that morning and ordered some breakfast and two glasses of milk. The stomach pain I had experienced the night before seemed to have subsided, and I convinced myself that I was letting nerves get the best of me. I ironed the red and white pinstriped suit that I would wear for the first day of the trial, and it wasn't long before my cell phone rang with Mark on the other end.

He was asking how my night was. I told him that I hadn't slept well but otherwise things were okay. He told me that he was at the courthouse and the first witnesses had testified, and that things were going well and my FBI escort would be there to pick me up around

11:45, but if I needed him to just call and he would come. I assured him I would be fine and finished getting ready. I had managed to avoid letting myself worry about testifying, as I knew that I was prepared and that I needed to just keep reminding myself of that. I hadn't expected Mark to come along with my escort, but I was relieved and happy to see him get out of the car. I asked what he was doing there, and he said that he wanted to make sure that I was all right and to have a familiar face at my side as I went through security, in case something went wrong as on the opening day of the Anderson court-martial. Luckily, this time I breezed through the courthouse security without incident. Mark took me into the conference room where we had done my witness prep to wait.

It was almost 2:00 before I was taken down to the courtroom. As we got into the elevator, I reminded myself over and over that I was ready and would get through this. When we exited the elevator, my escort said that I should just wait outside the doors of the courtroom until I was called. I nodded my head and clasped my hands, leaning against the wall in the hallway. It was just a few minutes later that Gurganus opened the doors and motioned for me to come in. I walked into the courtroom, and Gurganus whispered to me to take a few deep breaths, to concentrate on him, and to look toward the jury when I answered his questions. I walked by the rows of seats and saw a few reporters and a sketch artist. The courtroom was rather large and very modern. All of the evidence and exhibits had been scanned into a computer and were made available for viewing on monitors to each juror as well as the judge and witnesses.

The judge presiding over the trial was U.S. District Court Judge Edwin M. Kosik. Judge Kosik appeared firmly in control of his courtroom and proceedings. He was in his late sixties and had a friendly disposition in dealing with trial counsel and witnesses.

After I was sworn in, I turned and stepped up into the witness box and seated myself. My stomach started to gurgle, and I prayed that the microphone was not picking up the sound. I mustered all my will and tried to appear calm. I couldn't avoid glancing at Reynolds, who was seated next to his attorney, Joseph O'Brien, at the counsel table. Reynolds appeared markedly thinner than he had in the mug shot that I had seen well over a year before. Unlike Anderson, who avoided eye contact with me the first time we met in court, Reynolds stared straight at me. I remembered to concentrate on Gurganus and answer his questions while looking in the direction of the jury.

Gurganus began my direct examination by asking me to state my name, age, and where I resided. By the time of the Reynolds trial, I made every effort to state that I lived in Helena, Montana, to take attention away from Conrad and my family. Gurganus also asked questions about my education and employment history. When I had to answer that I had been a judge for over six years, Judge Kosik piped in, stating that he wasn't aware that I had been a judge and asked a few questions about my background as a judge and what kind of cases I had presided over. When he was done with his questions, he politely apologized to Gurganus, stating, "I apologize, Mr. Gurganus. I wasn't trying to do your job, but in all my years on the bench I can't remember having had a judge sitting as a witness." I just smiled, and the jury members laughed. It briefly eased the atmosphere in the courtroom.

As Gurganus proceeded with his examination of me, he moved into the questions that would allow the jury to understand me and why I had gotten into the field of cyber counterterrorism and intelligence. I explained to the jury how 9/11 had essentially radicalized me against terrorism, which evolved into the Internet work I had developed in subsequent years tracking individuals and groups involved in terrorist support and activities. When Gurganus asked about the

Anderson case, he kept his questions simple and focused, allowing me to answer as briefly as possible—knowing that O'Brien would likely try to delve deeper anyway.

Then came the questions about Reynolds—how I had come to know him on the Internet, the chronology of our email communications. Until now, I had avoided looking at the clock, and when I did I was surprised to see that it was almost 4:00. Gurganus told the court that he believed that he could finish his direct examination of me that day, but that unless the court wanted to continue testimony into the evening, O'Brien would have to begin his cross-examination the following morning. We were able to wrap up my direct testimony just after 5:30, and court adjourned until the next morning. By this time, I was beginning to feel sick again and was perspiring. When we exited the courtroom and Mark asked how it went, I said I thought it had gone well but wasn't feeling good, which he said he could tell because I looked pale. I said I would probably be fine and just needed to collect myself and get some rest for tomorrow, which would be the hard part of the trial. Because Mark was listed as a witness and expected to testify, we were staying in different hotels. When it was time for my escort to take me back to the hotel, Mark had already left the courthouse. My stomach was cramping pretty bad at this point, and all I wanted to do was get back to my room.

That night, the pain and cramping got progressively worse, and as much as I tried to relax and sleep, I couldn't. I didn't even attempt to eat anything because I had already started to vomit. In the early hours of the morning, I noticed blood in my vomit and became scared. I didn't want to cause a scene or bring any extra attention, so I just prayed and prayed for the strength to get through it. I lay in bed angry, asking God why he was letting me get sick right now. I felt like I was being punished.

I don't reach out to others for help easily, and I don't talk about my problems very often either. I internalize. That process of internalizing might have sustained me up to the point of the Anderson case, but after my life so drastically changed, the repression became too much. Now here I was again in the middle of another stressful case, and all of the years of repression appeared to finally be affecting my physical health.

Each hour that passed that night felt like an eternity, as I tried to get control of the vomiting. It was around 3:00 when I decided to take a long hot bath. After I got out of the tub, my body felt so tired that I lay under the covers wrapped in a bath towel, and I fell asleep for a couple of hours. Before I knew it the clock said 7:30 a.m., and I knew that I had to get out of that bed and dressed and make it through the day. I wasn't vomiting when I woke up, but my stomach was in pain. I managed to get myself ready and dressed and lay on the bed until 9:00, knowing I had to leave my room around 9:15. I kept powdering my face to hide the dark circles under my eyes. In the ride over to the courthouse I closed my eyes, and when we arrived in the parking garage, I was fighting the need to vomit. The FBI guys that were escorting me that morning noticed that I wasn't feeling well and asked if they could get me anything. I told them no, that I was afraid if I took anything it would just come right back up. I asked if Mark was at the courthouse, and they said they thought he had arrived earlier. When we got up to the conference room at the U.S. attorney's office, Mark was there, and he looked alarmed when he saw me. My escorts told him that I wasn't feeling well, and he asked if it was nerves or if I was sick. I told Mark that it had started getting bad after I got back to my room the night before and had vomited blood. I sat down on the couch along the wall, and within a few minutes we were both taken down to the courtroom and into a smaller room to wait. As we sat there, I asked Mark where the bathroom was and ran across the hall just in time to find an empty toilet slot and vomited. I didn't care if anyone was in there or heard me because I couldn't fight it anymore. I just sat there on the floor trying to stop vomiting.

A lady in the bathroom asked if she could get me anything or find someone to help me, and I said no. I didn't know it at the time, but the lady in the bathroom that morning was one of the reporters attending the trial. She knew who I was. When she left the bathroom, she passed the small witness room we had been in and told Mark that someone needed to help me. I heard a knock outside the door and Mark's voice, and told him I was trying to get it together. He came into the ladies' room and got me some wet paper towels to help me clean up. He said that he was going to get some water and that I should just sip it slowly so that I didn't get dehydrated. He put his arm around me and walked me out of the bathroom and told me he knew I could do this despite how sick I was feeling. I remember looking at him, seeing the resolve on his face. He said that they were waiting for me and went in and told Gurganus that I was ready.

I walked through the doors of the courtroom carrying the Styrofoam cup of water Mark had got me and held my head high as I walked past the jury and into the witness box. I looked at my surroundings and concentrated on Gurganus until O'Brien stood up and began his cross-examination.

As I sat there, I wondered, do I look sick? I felt calm enough for the moment, so maybe God had given me the reprieve I needed to get through this day. Either way, I wasn't going to fail. I would muster all the strength I had inside to keep it together on the witness stand.

O'Brien started off his questioning respectfully enough, and I wondered if his cross-examination would be as painless as Major Morse's in the Anderson case had been. To focus on for his questioning, O'Brien had selected a few of the emails the government had entered into evidence. As we had expected, Reynolds's defense would attempt to paint him in the same light as me—someone who went online to ferret out terrorists and threats. I was beginning to feel defensive with this line of questioning, and I fought myself not to react to attempts at provocation by O'Brien. But the farther he went down this path, the more it felt like a personal attack on my character and a way of belittling the importance of my work and my intentions.

O'Brien asked about any money I had received from the FBI over the years, and I proudly looked at the jury and told them that I had never received any compensation from the FBI other than reimbursement for expenses I had incurred and for translation work I had performed. O'Brien tried other angles to force me to admit I had received money for my work, and I answered his questions the same way each time—except for the last time, when I found myself pointing my finger at O'Brien and saying, "Asked and answered, Mr. O'Brien."

I immediately knew that I had let him get the best of me. My guard was worn down, and I had slipped. Judge Kosik said, "Ms. Rossmiller, I understand that you once ruled your own courtroom, but this is my courtroom, and I will admonish counsel as necessary." I apologized to Judge Kosik, stating that I was out of line and knew that I was as soon as the words left my mouth. I then turned to the jury and apologized as well. Gurganus stood up and asked the court to require Mr. O'Brien to move on with his questioning as I obviously didn't have any other way to answer his questions regarding any compensation received from the FBI. I sipped the last of my water. I couldn't imagine what was left for O'Brien to ask me, as we had covered the evidence already entered into the record, and he had asked all of the background questions that I imagined he possibly could. Thankfully, it was not long before he wrapped up his cross-examination, and Gurganus didn't have any rebuttal questions for me. When it was time to excuse me from the witness stand, Gurganus asked that I be excused from being held over subject to recall to the witness stand. O'Brien didn't object. Despite not feeling well, I remember wanting to scream, "I AM FREE!" I turned to Judge Kosik and thanked the court, then stepped down from the witness stand. Gurganus met me at the end of the jury box and walked me out of the courtroom. He thanked me and wished me well, telling me to go back to my room and feel better, and we shook hands. As I walked into the hall outside the courtroom, where Mark was standing, I said that I had made it through, as he predicted. He put his arm around me, patted my shoulder, and said we would talk later but that he was up next. As I watched Mark walk into the courtroom, I knew that if O'Brien tried to give him any hell he would get nowhere.

My FBI escorts met me at the elevator and took me down to the car. It was one of those moments when you know you have beaten the odds. My job as a witness was again done. I had survived the challenges, pressure, and stress of two high-profile terrorism cases. I vowed then and there that though I would never quit my cyber counterterrorism work, I would definitely change focus so that I might never find myself in this position again.

Proving his narcissism, Reynolds took the witness stand in his own defense. Gurganus fired off a barrage of questions about inconsistencies in things Reynolds had said and written, ranging from false diplomas, to exaggerations about his military and employment records, to glaring holes in his story that he was a private mercenary interested in taking down an al-Qaeda cell.

In his closing statement to the jury, Gurganus described Reynolds as "the guy who gets caught in the house saying he's not trying to burglarize it, but only testing the security system." Gurganus said, "It's silly."

"He was a guy looking for his day in the sun, looking to make his mark," O'Brien said. "He did his best, but maybe he didn't do it in the best way."

Reynolds's trial would last five days in all. His jury would deliberate only forty-five minutes before returning its verdict, handing down convictions on five of the six counts in the indictment. He would be sentenced to thirty years in federal prison for his crimes on November 25, 2007. I felt an immediate sense of relief, thinking, "Well, there's another one locked away for the rest of his life. I am happy." Though I had returned home to Montana the day before the verdict was announced, my health was deteriorating. The stomach pain and nausea I was experiencing in Pennsylvania during the trial had not subsided. Over the weekend following the trial, I continued to get worse, and the pain became excruciating by Monday morning. I was taken to the emergency room at St. Peter's hospital in Helena and was diagnosed with two kidney stones and a bleeding ulcer.

In the end, Michael Reynolds was just another narcissistic social misfit who believed that everyone and everything had thwarted the greatness he believed he deserved. In his mind, society, his family, and the government had all failed him—but he hadn't failed. In the end, the sociological and psychological similarities between Michael Reynolds and Ryan Anderson and what each intended to do to harm their country link them as kindred damaged souls who sought the greatness they believed they had been denied, only to find themselves infamous.

The stress and pressure of the Reynolds trial, coupled with the tension of being away from my family, had taken its toll. I found myself paying a high price for trying to balance my new job at the attorney general's office with my family, my Internet work, and preparing for and going through the Reynolds trial. To say I was pushed to the max would be a vast understatement.

I decided after the Reynolds trial that there was no way in hell I was going to end up in another court case. The intense pressure that I found myself under as a witness in a high-profile case and how that affected my life as well as the lives of my family was not something I wanted to be a part of again. Though the Anderson and Reynolds cases were important cases for our country and they were successfully prosecuted, I resent how my life and family were disrupted and how my life changed. I resented having to accept my new life. I didn't plan to give up, but I knew that I couldn't continue going down this path. I would need to find a way to continue my work that would allow me to remain out of the chain of evidence that would put me in the middle of another high-profile case.

Once I made this decision to avoid cases that would put me into another prosecution, the answers I needed were much more simple. Now, when I am working on a threat related to an individual present in the U.S. or subject to its jurisdiction, rather than work the communications of the case where the evidence is created, I now hand off the information and target to the FBI at the earliest stage. In the years since the Anderson case when the FBI was still finding its way and cutting its teeth as the U.S.'s domestic intelligence agency in charge of cyber terrorism, there are now FBI agents and trained analysts who are positioned to take an early handoff from me and run with it.

After the Reynolds trial, the FBI went public about my work for the first time. Special Agent in Charge Tim Fuhrman (Salt Lake City Division) told an Associated Press reporter, "To her credit, she's very humble about her role and she should be recognized for the integral role she played in [the Reynolds] case and other cases."

I was humbled by his statement. A lot of what I do is misunder-stood or not understood at all. Some people say I'm a crackpot with too much time on my hands, or a vigilante. Because there are so many delicate and sensitive things that go along with my role, I want people to understand the choices that I made and their consequences.

CHAPTER TWELVE

AL-QAEDA COMES TO MONTANA

In July of 2006, I was in Helena, where I had stayed overnight that Thursday night after meeting with Mark on the Reynolds case as well as other matters I was working on at the time. The next morning, while I was busy getting ready to pack up and head home to my family in Conrad, I noticed the message notification light on my cell phone blinking. I dialed my voice mail and was surprised to hear the message waiting for me.

It was from Mike Galloway, one of my Conrad city police officers. Galloway said there had been an incident late the previous evening that appeared to be a threat targeted at me, and to contact him or whoever was on duty that morning at the police department or the sheriff's department. I had just finished blow-drying my hair and dressing before I listened to the voicemail message, and I wondered what could be involved. The telephone threats following the Anderson case back in 2004 had diminished, and I had not heard any updates from the FBI or CSIS, the FBI's partner in Canada. I sat down on the hotel bed and thought for a few minutes before I made any calls. I was sure that none of the operational IDs I had used since that time had been compromised, as I had changed my methods in the aftermath of the Anderson case. I also wondered why the voice message had been left by Officer Galloway rather than Mark. One of the things that the FBI had implemented for me after the Anderson case was a protocol involving local law enforcement in my area in conjunction with the FBI (that is, Mark) and officials with Customs and Border Patrol at the Sweet Grass border crossing—the nearest crossing between Montana and Alberta, Canada.

I decided that I had better not waste more time speculating and called Galloway's cell phone. He answered and asked where I was and if I was okay. After I assured him that I was fine but was concerned about his message, he explained that shortly after 10:00 the night before the highway patrol and sheriff's department were dispatched to a vehicle accident on a desolate gravel road outside of Valier—about twenty-five miles north of Conrad. When law enforcement and emergency officials arrived, they found a Ryder rental truck that had apparently overcorrected a turn, causing it to roll down a ravine. There were four individuals in the truck. Two were severely injured, and two had suffered minor injuries. All four were taken to the Conrad Hospital for medical attention. The severely injured were flown from Conrad to the trauma center in Great Falls. Galloway relayed that one had suffered severe burns and the other had suffered a broken back and neck. The burn victim, I learned later, was eventually transferred to a Salt Lake City burn center.

Officer Galloway explained that the four men had apparently come into Montana from Canada. They had raised suspicion, as all four had dark skin and claimed to be Muslims but none appeared to be of Arab ethnicity. The four men had valid U.S. visas, but their passports revealed that they hailed from multiple nations. Two were from Eritrea, in East Africa; one was from Suriname, in South America; and the last was from Bahrain, in the Persian Gulf.

Apparently, at the accident scene, GPS transmitting equipment and wireless laptops were found scattered around the wrecked Ryder truck. Disassembled weapons were discovered in boxes that had been covered up with T-shirts and other items. There were also a significant number of Korans littering the scene.

Given what had happened, Galloway said, "We need to determine that you and the family aren't in any harm. And considering the terrorism work you do, until we rule out there is no viable threat, why don't you stay in Helena another night? Hopefully by tomorrow we'll have it all sorted out." He also told me that a couple of the officers had gone over to the house to talk to Randy and that he and the kids would go out to his mother's place for the day. I wondered, at that moment, why Randy hadn't called and tried to talk to me that morning, but I figured that he had probably been busy getting everyone together to leave.

I stayed in Helena until Sunday morning, when the two men who had not been badly injured were taken by federal authorities to Seattle. My family and I returned to Conrad to find that the FBI had requested a car be posted outside our home until further notice.

I spoke to Randy later on the same day of my conversation with Galloway, and learned why he hadn't called me that morning. He was angry that my work was again posing a threat to our family and putting us all in danger—and "the whole town of Conrad as well," as he said that morning. He started to point out that, just as had happened when the Anderson trial brought me national notoriety, the locals wouldn't understand and couldn't understand my actions because my activities were so far removed from the everyday life in a small Montana town. He was also concerned about how news of this situation would affect his business. His resentment was obvious. I felt the guilt building inside me. I couldn't blame him. Randy was told he couldn't be in our home—he was fuming mad that he was asked to get the kids and leave. Randy would tell friends and family that, for a while after this incident, he slept with one eye open.

I WOULD LATER LEARN that, when questioned at the Conrad Hospital, the two men who were not badly injured claimed they were traveling with the Van's Warped Tour, a Lollapalooza-like traveling music show, selling band T-shirts and trinkets. At the time of the accident, the Warped Tour was traveling through Montana on its way to Washington. The men, it seemed, had branched off from the tour and traveled into Canada. However, when crossing back into Montana, they did not use any of the official U.S.-Canadian border crossings. Instead, they simply drove into Montana using the GPS equipment to navigate the open and unsecured gravel roads along the Montana-Alberta border, which stretches a distance of 545 miles. After law enforcement completed their search of the men's laptop computers and examination of their GPS equipment, I would learn that my home address, in addition to the address for the courthouse in Conrad, was preprogrammed into their equipment—establishing that I was, in fact, their target that day.

When the injured men arrived at the Conrad Hospital, one of the men had been clutching his laptop computer tightly, refusing to let it go. At first, law enforcement tried to get the men to consent to a search of their belongings, which was refused. But considering all the red flags the suspects had raised, obtaining a search warrant wasn't much of a problem.

Though all four men were wearing Western-style clothing at the time of the accident, when medical personnel at the Conrad Hospital tried to cut away the clothing of the two men who weren't badly injured, in order to check them over, each was found to be wearing what appeared to be a male chastity belt—a personal garment worn by fundamentalist Muslims representing the preservation of one's virginity—underneath his jeans. When the hospital staff attempted to remove the garments to continue with their examinations, the men refused further medical treatment. They did not wish to be touched by "unclean hands," and especially those of the female members of the medical staff. After refusing further treatment, the two men requested that law enforcement return their personal property. Their conduct at the Conrad Hospital, the disparity between their outward appearance as Westerners and their apparent practice of fundamentalist Islam, their claims to being traveling salesmen, their lack of a reasonable explanation for their illegal entry into Montana from Alberta, as well as the presence of GPS tracking equipment connected with laptops and copies of the Koran covered up by rock band T-shirts and music tradeshow trinkets were all causes for suspicion and alarm.

I wondered then, and I still wonder, whether the threat these four men presented resulted from the leak of my undercover identity during the Anderson court-martial. Though more than three years had passed since that time, knowing that al-Qaeda and its followers were patient and trained to lay low and quiet for lengthy periods of time, I should not have become complacent.

I often shudder to think what would have happened if they hadn't been such bumbling drivers on a gravel road in a rental truck. They had weapons, and their GPS was pointed toward my family's home. If they hadn't wrecked their truck that day, I might not be here, or,

God forbid, my family could have been harmed. I've always felt guilty about that.

Randy was furious, and I didn't blame him. At the time, I thought, let's just get through this and move on. We'll let the FBI do what they do. But Randy asked, "What if they dispatch another cell, and they make it here? Then what happens?"

When he said that he had had enough, I didn't realize at first what that actually meant. Everything that I was doing had changed me, and it had changed our family life. And sometimes it seemed like the more I did, the less control I had. In hindsight, this incident was a turning point in our lives and in our marriage. It was a page I wish had never been turned, as it marked the beginning of the downward spiral of our relationship and the eventual end of our marriage. When things are just starting to go bad, we don't or can't see everything that we stand to lose. Though I was struggling through this period of time, I found sanctuary within the world of my computer and with the recognition that comes with my work.

CHAPTER THIRTEEN

WHAT IS A HERO?

With each year that has passed since 9/11, our collective sense of complacency, both in the U.S. and abroad, has grown. If history teaches us anything, it is that we should not lose sight of historical events that have impacted and changed the world. Historically, societal complacency has enabled history to repeat itself, and if we fail to learn the painful lessons from what has happened, we are doomed to suffer it again.

In the years after 9/11, I found myself frustrated and discouraged with how news of the war was being reported to the public. There was so much negative media that I felt people should be reminded that the actions the U.S. government was taking were being taken to protect us from harm. As a counterbalance to negative stories such as Abu Ghraib, car bombings, beheadings, and all the atrocities that come with war which only feed negative feelings and images about the United States both at home and abroad, I thought we also deserved to learn of some of the successes that were not being covered by the media. After all, the American people pay the same taxes, and our brave soldiers shed the same blood on behalf of the United States that my grandparents and earlier ancestors did during the other wars and conflicts that have shaped our history as a country.

During World War II, the U.S. public was bombarded with pro-war messages through posters, newsreels, and photographs in the press. This public information campaign was directed by the United States Office of War Information (OWI), which was created to con-solidate government information services and coordinate the release of war news. The OWI worked to promote patriotism, warn about foreign spies, and recruit soldiers for the war effort. The office also established an overseas branch that launched a large-scale informa-tion and propaganda campaign abroad, educating the public about vital aspects of the defense effort through radio, the print press, and newsreels. These media reports informed the public not only about setbacks and losses, but also about positive news and information from the battlefronts in the war.

Since the War on Terror began in October 2001, an imbalance in news reporting has denied the news consumers the opportunity to weigh the pros and cons of the war and to develop informed views and opinions.

By June 2006, I realized that the successful results from the cases I'd worked on, which had occurred mostly offshore, could be offered to the public as evidence of the positive results of the War on Ter-ror that the government was not releasing or that the media was not reporting on. Of course, the wars of today and tomorrow are unlike traditional wars. They occur not between soldiers on a battlefield but between nations, paramilitary and terrorist groups, and the wildly differing ideologies that characterize our world. In the age of the In-ternet, the War on Terror is a virtual war fought in the theater of cy-berspace as well as on the ground where the enemy is nested. And it's a taller order to get a whole nation of people behind a war like that.

In the wake of such scandals as Abu Ghraib, the controversial rendition of enemy combatants, and the alleged military torture and treatment of detainees at the U.S. Guantánamo Bay detention facility in Cuba, I decided that the American public could use some news about the successes of the War on Terror. My decision was influenced by what I perceived as the media controlling the information the public was getting, in what I felt had become an ongoing campaign to adversely affect public perception of the U.S. military and intelligence community's roles in the war.

To be clear, I also faulted the U.S. government for not taking measures to share more of the good-news stories with the public.

I knew I was in a unique position to help change that.

In June of 2006, after clearing the completed cases I had worked on with the FBI—Michael Reynolds was in a Pennsylvania jail and would be charged for his crimes in December—I had embarked on my own campaign to provide public awareness of some of the success stories I had personally been involved with, and to counter all the negative headlines.

Of course, in taking these cases public, certain facts and details such as names, dates, and locations had to be changed to protect myself and my undercover identities, as well as the integrity of my partnership with the government and FBI.

My other objective with the public awareness campaign was to show the public that private individuals like me, with specialized training and skill sets, could contribute to the global fight against terrorism.

The media outlets that I chose for my public awareness campaign were selected for both their domestic and international reach. I made television appearances on *Good Morning America,* CNN's *Paula Zahn Now,* and the *BBC World News.* The print media outlets I chose included the *Washington Post, Houston Chronicle,* and *Philadelphia*

Inquirer here in the U.S., as well as the *London Telegraph* and *YOU Magazine* in the U.K.

In selecting the cases to include in my campaign, I wanted to highlight the landscape and depth of the complexities that the U.S. was facing on the two fronts—physical and virtual—of the War on Terror.

One of the cases I included was that of a fourteen-year-old boy in the Philippines who was posting messages in the jihadist forums in April of 2005, reaching out to al-Qaeda to help him join his brothers:

> Assalaamu alakum:
>
> I am a 14 year old student in the Philippines. I study in a Cathlic school whee a lot of nonsense is pervasive. I would like to carry out Jihad. How should I go about it? I have some knowledge on the Filipino Martial Arts and Karate. Though I have experience handling guns, I do not have any firearms at home.
>
> > Please help me
> >
> > May Allah bless us all in our future endeavors

Using my undercover alias of Abu Musa, I wrote back:

> In the Name of Allah, the Benificent, the Merciful, and the prayer and the greeting on the militants imam our master Mohamed peace be upon him and till now,
>
> > my brother in Allah,
> >
> > I am Abu Musa from a blue Jordan and I come to you through our sheikh Al-Zarqawi may Allah keep . . . I am with the group of the brotherhood who find the way to the paradise for jihad . . . . I contact you for joining to the fight of the brothers in the jihad . . . i warn you now of the danger with talk of these issues on the Internet . . . email is safe for us . . . i will help you to a secret place for training the jihad. abu _ musa7777@yahoo.com . . . therefore i hope you take the care and caution and avoid the cross salves and unbelievers everywhere . . .

your brother in Allah

Abu Musa

This case, though painful to contemplate, showed how effective the Internet is in reaching out to youths looking for a purpose and path in life. Fourteen is, in fact, a prime and impressionable age for Islamic radicalization as well as recruitment.

Another case I selected for inclusion in my campaign was that of Black Flag, the individual who claimed to be an associate professor in nuclear physics at a Middle Eastern university. I chose the case of Black Flag because, given the confirmation from my colleague in Canada who is an educated and trained nuclear physicist, the depth of the information Black Flag was offering an alleged al-Qaeda operative was alarming, as was how easy it would have been for an individual with his background and experience to succeed in establishing contact with al-Qaeda through the Internet.

The final two cases I chose for my campaign were those of Anderson and Reynolds, to show the American public how even U.S. citizens or members of the U.S. military, wanting to bring harm and destruction to their own country, could easily utilize the Internet for purposes of carrying out their plans of attack.

For the most part, my public awareness campaign was well received, and I got more feedback from the public than I had anticipated I would. I felt the campaign had tapped into a public sentiment of support for the War on Terror that the media had disregarded in its overall coverage of the war.

MY FIRST OFFICIAL RECOGNITION for my work in pioneering the field of cyber counterintelligence came in October of 2006, when I was honored with the Middle East Forum's American

Hero Award. The Middle East Forum is a think tank that works to identify threats arising out of the Middle East as well as to promote American interests in the Middle East in the areas of education, sponsored projects, and philanthropy. The MEF is run by Dr. Daniel Pipes, an internationally renowned expert on the Middle East and terrorism-related issues. I had come to the attention of Dr. Pipes as a result of the Ryan Anderson case. When news of my involvement became public and a popular news story back in 2004, Dr. Pipes and the MEF were the first to recognize the importance of the work I had done, and put up a page on the MEF's website entitled, "Shannen Rossmiller—American Hero." I had known of Dr. Pipes and the MEF very early on in my quest to understand the threat of terrorism, having often visited and utilized the vast archives and resources on the organization's site. So I was stunned to wake up one day to an email from a friend providing me a link to the page honoring my work. Since that time, I have come to count Dr. Pipes and the wonderful people of the MEF as treasured friends and colleagues.

At first, it was hard to conceptualize and bear all that being a hero means. It is a measure of honor and respect for duties and actions performed by one without self-interest, so of course it's a good and honorable thing. However, I am by nature a humble person, and I'm a bit uncomfortable being labeled a hero. I am a person who was raised to know the difference between right and wrong and to always try to do the right things. Though I have made my share of mistakes, I can stand tall and say with honesty that, regarding my antiterrorism and intelligence work, I have done the things I have done for the right reasons and with the right intentions.

Another highlight came in March of 2009, when I was honored to receive the Congressional Medal of Honor Society's "Above and Beyond Citizens Award" for the State of Montana. This beautiful award was bestowed on me by an organization made up of soldiers who fought for our country, protecting all of the rights and freedoms on which America was founded. They were recognized for their bravery in the face of danger and harm, and to be recognized by them is priceless to me. Coming from a body of true American heroes, it felt like the strongest testament to the work I had done and the pain and sacrifices I had endured.

CONCLUSION

A CALL TO
PATRIOTISM

I continued to work at the attorney general's office until May of 2009, when I decided to resign my position to work full-time on national security and intelligence projects. My health had also become an obstacle: I was experiencing ongoing problems with ulcers, and I was running out of steam, no longer having the strength to commute between Helena and Conrad and to continue both my paying job with the attorney general's office and my unpaid work as a cyber spy.

Deciding to leave my career in law to pursue the unknown future of the security and intelligence field was a hard call to make, but I needed the challenge, and my health was telling me I was at a crossroads. I felt then, as I do today, that I did the right thing. I had helped to pioneer a new field of intelligence that didn't exist before 2001, and in doing so I was able to incorporate all of my talents, interests, and skill sets in one job. And though I would leave my job with the attorney general's office, I have never really left the law behind. I had come to find that my legal background was one of the critical foundations that allowed me to do the level of credible anti-terrorism and intelligence work I did, so I wasn't too downhearted. It was a new horizon for me, and a challenge that I was relishing.

Back in 2004, at the end of the Anderson trial, I had met a man who entered my life to save me from the media madness that had ensued as a result of that case. Tom Colbert, the owner of an independent media consulting company known as IRD (Industry Research and Development), took pity on the scared woman from Montana that he had seen in TV news reports on the Anderson case. After I returned home, Tom contacted me and offered to step in and take control of all of my media requests. In the years after the Anderson case, Tom and his family have become like a second family to me, and I honestly cannot say I would have survived this journey without Tom.

Tom became a partner in my later efforts to develop a civilian cyber corps. We started a national security company called AC-CIO (Advanced Cyber Counter Intelligence Operations) and hired a national security attorney in Washington, D.C., Mark Zaid. From May 2009 to the present, Tom and I have consulted with several of the large defense contracting companies, including Boeing, Lockheed Martin, and L-3, to name a few. We have also traveled around the country giving lectures, and I have spoken at several national security and intelligence conferences.

The move from my day job was a gamble that ultimately allowed me to be free. The change in careers offered a more relaxed pace that has helped my health rebound. For the first time in several years, I was healthy and feeling my energy coming back.

Though I had not anticipated I would ever leave my career in the law, I also never anticipated that the intelligence and national security work I have done for the past nine years would evolve into a viable opportunity for a midlife career change. I am proud of the work I have done over the years. Having said all that, when I reflect on the loss of my privacy and private life, my marriage and family life, I still have feelings of regret and grief. Though there are days when dealing with these losses is difficult, over time the memories have become less painful. I have been asked by many people over the years if I would change anything that I have done. I always respond that, of course, you can't go back, but I certainly would have done some things differently if life afforded us the benefit of hindsight as foresight. When it comes to the work, though, I know I would have done the cyber counterintelligence work, and for all the same reasons. The life God has chosen for me has a purpose, and I try to remember that when I find myself grieving for what once was.

Living alone and working during the week in Helena is a lonely existence. When I first started working in Helena during the week in 2006 when I was working at the attorney general's office, it was hard to be away from my family. Working and living away from my family was an existence that I never anticipated. I miss the family dynamic. At times, I find myself missing Randy and our marriage and all that we had as a family in the days before 9/11. But in my journey into the world of Internet terrorism, I changed as a person, along with my interests and professional focus. But, Randy changed as well. In hindsight, it is easy to see how we grew apart from each other, and in the end what happened was almost inevitable. Supporting me and my Internet work, and setting aside any resentment he bore toward me for the changes in our marriage and family became too much for Randy. The catalyst was none other than 9/11—a day I took personally that changed my life. Randy never made that leap with me. Like most Americans in the years since 9/11, he moved on, but I just never did.

I remember once I told Randy I had this dream of going to Pakistan. I had begun trying to plan a trip to explore actual places I know so well—virtually. However, just as had happened with my dream years earlier of joining the National Guard, Randy would not have it. I didn't even make it to first base, as Randy's response echoed what I had heard several times before: "You're not going to Pakistan, Shannen. Over my dead body! You're a mother with three kids, and you wouldn't last a day as a blond woman just getting off the plane—whether you believe you are Super Burka Woman or not! Don't be a fool." But I do think about traveling to that part of the world, and I will one day—maybe when I am a little less active with my antiterrorism work.

Again, Randy was right. I wanted nothing more than to be a part of that culture and explore that world. Of course, I would have had to dye my hair so I wouldn't stick out like a sore thumb. My biggest dream is to take a tour of the Silk Road that travels from China, down into Pakistan, Afghanistan, and into Iran and Iraq. I feel like I've been to all of these places and know so much about them from my computer. But one day, I truly would like to leave the United States and just go, to soak in and breathe the air there.

In late 2007, I was asked to participate in a Department of Defense (DoD) study on the process and effect of the Islamist radicalization process, and how to spot red flags and warnings. Again, the catalyst for this request was the Anderson case. Anderson's case provided the closest and most complete available picture into the radicalization process of one of DoD's own. The study was entitled "The Radicalization of Members of the DoD," and it provided findings and recommendations to provide military administrators and supervisors with a resource and tool to guide them on how to spot the red flags an individual at risk within its ranks might exhibit. The study was completed in August of 2008 and disseminated not only within the military intelligence community but to the U.S. intelligence community at large.

Then, on November 5, 2009, Major Nidal Malik Hasan, an Army psychiatrist who had recently transferred from the Walter Reed Army Hospital in Virginia to Fort Hood, Texas, went on a shooting rampage on the base, killing thirteen and injuring twenty-nine American military and civilian base personnel. In the aftermath of the Fort Hood attack, a startling amount of information began to trickle out regarding overt actions and statements from Major Hasan, indicating that he had become radicalized under the extremist ideology espoused by al-Qaeda. Many sources suggested Hasan had been exhibiting these red flags for more than three years prior to the attack. Yet the Army took no actions to deal with the growing threat he presented.

The Army also claimed that there were no tools or resources available to help them deal with the problem of radicalization in general, and felt that Hasan was "untouchable" because he was a Muslim. They feared that any attempt to address his behavior might be construed as prejudice against him as a Muslim or the Islamic faith generally. I was outraged listening to the Army and DoD attempting to whitewash the Fort Hood tragedy and excuse their negligence, when it appeared that virtually everyone who had worked with or knew Hasan had been aware of his beliefs. The public record includes several documented instances when Major Hasan's behavior had merited threat assessment and inquiry. Some of the behavioral cues and red flags Major Hasan presented that were known to Army officials in advance of the attack on Fort Hood include the following:

- In 2008 and 2009 Army doctors discussed "red flags"
  regarding Major Hasan's behavior as it related to his

mental health and fitness to be treating vulnerable soldiers returning from war.

- Concerns over Hasan being psychotic or the potential for a fratricide incident were discussed.
- Colleagues repeatedly reported their concerns about him.
- He justified suicide bombings in an Internet posting.
- He lectured colleagues using the rhetoric of jihad.
- Hasan openly talked about "adverse events" if Muslims were not allowed to leave military service.
- He repeatedly sought counsel from Anwar al-Awlaki, a radical American-Yemeni cleric and al-Qaeda supporter.
- Hasan tried to convert some of his patients to Islam—many of them soldiers troubled by their near-fatal experiences with jihadists.
- He printed business cards that made no mention of his military service but instead identified him as an "SOA," a soldier of Allah.
- Hasan stated openly that he was a Muslim first and an American second.
- Hasan attended a Middle East terrorism conference in January 2009.

Every instance cited above represented an opportunity where the Army could have taken proper action against Hasan but failed to do so. Based on all that has been reported in the media since the Fort Hood attacks, had the Army, and to a lesser extent the FBI, taken action, any one of these missed opportunities could have prevented the Fort Hood massacre. I strongly believed that the American public was entitled to an explanation of how someone with a history of such threat-related behavior was allowed to remain in the Army, much less continue with his duties as an Army psychiatrist.

By November 19, 2009, I had heard enough of the claims that there had been no resources available for the Army to deal with Hasan. I decided to inform the public that there was in fact a 2008 DoD study commissioned, completed, and disseminated to the Army and intelligence community at large that not only studied the issue of radicalization but provided findings and recommendations on how administrators and supervisory personnel could deal with an individual suspected of radicalization. I had scheduled an appearance on CNN's *Anderson Cooper 360* to discuss the DoD study and its availability to the Army well in advance of the Fort Hood attack. My position was that had the Army followed and utilized the DoD study, those who were killed and injured at the hands of Major Hasan at Fort Hood might have been saved. Appearing on the show with me was Michigan Rep. Peter Hoekstra, a member of the House Committee on Intelligence. Rep. Hoekstra backed me up, discussing the DoD's and the military's poor understanding of the threat of extremist radicalization, and how the Fort Hood massacre proved the issue would need to be investigated further if we were to prevent future incidents involving radicalization. My speaking out on the study was little comfort to those families who lost their loved ones, but I felt that I could not sit in silence and let the talking heads cover up and excuse what the Army, DoD, and FBI's blindness to what was in front of them had allowed at Fort Hood.

I had never intended to be a whistleblower on the issue of radicalization. It was simply the right thing to do, since I had participated in the 2008 DoD study and those families of the thirteen people who were killed that day deserved to know that something could have and should have been done to prevent their unspeakable losses.

In December of 2007, I had been invited to give the keynote speech at the SANS Cyber Security Conference in Washington, D.C. While I was in D.C. to give the speech, I was asked to meet with R. James Woolsey, a former director of the Central Intelligence Agency, for a brunch meeting at my hotel, the Weston, in Georgetown to discuss my accomplishments and counterintelligence work. The morning of the Woolsey meeting, I was a nervous wreck. I couldn't imagine that my work had taken me to a level where the former CIA director wanted to actually meet me. Woolsey arrived with one of his former Booz Allen Hamilton colleagues, Melissa Hathaway, who was then serving as the cyber operations director under Michael Hayden, the then-director of National Intelligence at the Office of the Director of National Intelligence.

Though he is incredibly accomplished, I found Jim Woolsey to be a humble, intelligent, down-to-earth man. He was funny and animated, telling pointed jokes I could relate to and appreciate. I was also happy to find out that he and I shared similar small-town backgrounds. He was at ease talking about growing up in a small prairie town in Oklahoma, and how he won a Rhodes Scholarship, and about his time in law school and eventual appointment and confirmation as the director of the CIA. He said to me, "People who come from little places like we do—the world is such a big place, and I can relate so much to your environment and where you came from and who you have come to be." We discussed our respective "where were you on 9/11" stories, and I felt blessed that he had shared his experience with me.

At one point during brunch, director Woolsey told me, "Wouldn't it be nice if we could clone your skill set." I was flattered, but I had no idea how this might be done. Woolsey went on to explain his idea of a national cyber corps made up of individuals and experts with talents and skill sets in the different areas that allowed me to be successful.

He explained that he felt my background in the law had served me extremely well in the work I had done as a private citizen and one not beholden to bureaucracy. He also expounded on the importance of understanding behavioral science, language and culture, and technology, as well as how to develop effective undercover identities, all as important areas to develop in the national cyber corps. I immediately understood. Melissa Hathaway went so far as to say, "Frankly, we've tried to do what you do and we can't."

We discussed the various threats facing the U.S. and world, and I spent more time than I had knowledge to keep up with him about Iran. I found him to be inspiring and interesting—a true role model and moral man. Our discussions kept circling around to the cyber corps concept, and as the meeting went on I came to see the potential value of a private national force to augment and enhance government functions in the world of cyber intelligence, where bureaucracy and traditional government structure can impede acting in real time, which is often what's required to make a difference. Earlier that year, the Air Force had attempted to create a similar unit they called the "Air Force Cyber Command," but it was implemented only provisionally and disbanded in October of 2008.

I mentioned the frustrations I encountered with government bureaucracy in the course of my work, and said that there had to be some protocols and procedures established to allow the intelligence agencies to partner with the private sector, as the FBI had done with me, to meet the challenge of threats developing in real time. I explained my long-held belief that if al-Qaeda and all it encompasses is to be defeated, governments must develop a better understanding of the ways the organization and its affiliates use the Internet and technology. Intelligence agencies must be allowed to think outside the box and incorporate creative strategies that allow them to anticipate where the terrorists might next carve their path on the Internet. Western governments still lag behind al-Qaeda in cyber warfare. If they do not catch up, they will never gain the upper hand in the War on Terror.

I left the meeting with Jim Woolsey convinced that I was the right person to advance his concept of a national cyber corps. I soon began sketching out a structure of what I envisioned for a cyber corps and how it could function in the private sector while partnering with the seventeen government intelligence agencies that make up the U.S. intelligence community. The hardest part would be finding the funding. I continue in this effort to this day. In January 2009, I officially announced the cyber corps concept as the keynote speaker at the FBI's first ever International Conference on Cyber Security, which was hosted by New York City's Fordham University.

Over the years that I had worked and brought my cases to the FBI, I had the opportunity to watch it grow and find its way into the world of cyber intelligence and security. I remember back to November of 2003, when I first brought what became the Ryan Anderson case to the FBI's Great Falls field office, only to find that they didn't have the Internet and had to use the public library down the street to go online. I was proud to see how far the Bureau had come.

The ICCS conference invited delegations from countries around the world, consisting of experts in the cyber security and intelligence fields, to congregate and discuss the various issues and threats they faced in their respective parts of the world.

Over five hundred handpicked experts from forty countries, representing law enforcement, intelligence, academia, and the private security industry, attended the weeklong conference from January 5–9, 2009, to catalog the latest global cyber threats and to develop combative techniques and strategies.

Being invited to be the keynote speaker at the ICCS conference was such an honor for me, illustrating how far I had come from the day in November of 2001 when I first learned about the terrorist Internet sites from a CNN news report.

The ICCS conference occurred just a little over a month after the attacks in Mumbai, India, that killed 164 and injured more than 300. It was an opportune time to have an international conversation. At the conference, I meet the Abu Dhabi delegation, who were a wonderful bunch. I had never met anyone from Abu Dhabi, though I had virtually operated from that country at times. I was surprised and amused to learn that they had heard of me and my work but had wondered whether I was real or just a product personality created by the U.S. government for purposes of propaganda. The fact that anyone had even considered such a thought . . .

Throughout the conference, the ICCS organizers encouraged interaction and open communication in an effort to find true common ground. The Internet, after all, is global; the boundaries of normal life are irrelevant there. The NSA, CIA, FBI, and DHS were all in attendance, along with private defense contractors.

At the end of the conference, I delivered the keynote speech explaining my methods and how an active network for cyber sleuths might help formalize them. I outlined each of the major challenges confronting our nation's security—including defeating global terrorism, countering weapons of mass destruction, ensuring the security of the homeland, transforming defense capabilities, fostering cooperation with other global powers, and promoting global economic growth—and explained how each has an embedded counterintelligence imperative. Terrorists and tyrants, foreign adversaries and economic competitors, I explained, all engage in a range of intelligence activities directed against us in order to advance their interests and defeat U.S. objectives. Too often, they have been successful. Collectively, they present strategic threats to the nation's security and prosperity. The United States, I continued, requires a national, systematic perspective and coherent policies to counter such threats, including a strategic counterintelligence response.

I have been told that what is compelling about my story, and the twists and turns it has taken, is where I ended up. When I first went to college, I wanted to study criminal justice and behavioral sciences to become and FBI profiler. But I never did. I also had planned to go to law school and become a criminal attorney. But I never did. Instead of taking the traditional paths toward a career incorporating my interest in the law, criminal behavior, and behavioral sciences and profiling, I found my own way to achieve success in these areas. I never lost those interests or gave up the goals. I just did it my own way. Yet, despite bucking the traditional courses, I managed to supersede and transcend my original ambitions.

In counterintelligence, the goal is to collect intelligence information to prevent acts of terrorism and to work proactively within the law to frustrate the activities of terrorists. It's not something you do for personal glory, since while your failures are apparent to all, your successes are usually known only to a few. That said, defeating terrorism must remain one of our intelligence community's core objectives, as widely dispersed terrorist networks will present one of the most serious challenges to U.S. national security interests at home and abroad. We also cannot forget that our terrorist enemies are patient, persistent, imaginative, adaptive, and dangerous opponents. Let's face it: Terrorism, technology, and homeland security are now a part of our daily vocabulary. Over the past decade and more, America has been changing its form and function to fit the new priorities presented in a post-9/11 world to fight the structural realities that global terrorism presents. In this capacity, it is my hope that we can help build a stronger and safer nation and world. The challenges we face are fierce. But standing together, we can accomplish the tasks that lie ahead.

Since 2001, I have continued to challenge myself to outthink and outmaneuver our enemy by forging new and untested methods in the field of cyber counterintelligence, in order to always gain the upper hand in an operation. Whenever I set out to take out any terrorist operative or group, I always have one main motivating factor in sight: to prevent the individual or group from doing harm.

I left the audience with these strong words, that in some manner has become my doctrine regarding the War on Terror and the terrorist enemy:

> We cannot forget Afghanistan and the sacrifices and battles that continue there. We cannot forget the battles in Iraq and sacrifices and battles that continue there. We must never forget that our fight for freedom did not end in Kabul. It will not end along the banks of the Tigris and Euphrates in Iraq. The fight continues here—on America's streets, off our shores, and in the skies above. We must never forget that we are in a war to preserve life and liberty. We must never forget that our enemies are ruthless fanatics, who seek to murder innocent men, women, and children to achieve their twisted goals. We must never forget that in the struggle between the forces of freedom and the ideology of hate, our challenge in this war against terrorism is to adapt and anticipate, to think outside the box to outmaneuver our enemies. And most importantly, no matter how far removed we get from the tragic day of September 11, we must never become complacent in our fight against the evil that terrorism represents.

On September 20, 2001, President George W. Bush called on the American public and the people of the world to join in a global coalition to fight against terror. That speech was unique because it called for a different type of war. It asked for a nontraditional war for which there was no existing road map or strategy for our military, law enforcement, and diplomatic and intelligence services to draw from. It was nearly impossible to envision what it would take to prosecute a war against terrorism, let alone what success would look like. In this calling, President Bush sought to draw together our allies in a global, coordinated effort to end terrorism as a legitimate political tool. When President Bush launched the War on Terror, some private citizens heard it as a personal call to arms. I am one of those people.

As we have all seen since September 11, brave men and women both in the civilian sector and in uniform have answered our leaders' call for justice. Sworn to defend the Constitution and our liberties, and motivated by the memories of September 11, they, like me, live each day by a code of honor, duty, and country. Although I am not in uniform as one of them, I fight their fight every day and have known many of them well enough to say that my story is, in many respects, their story.

When I reflect on what set me down my path, I realize I was flying blind at the time, with no sense of where this pursuit might take me. I was simply searching for an understanding and answers for what happened to our country on 9/11.

What I didn't know at the time I began my journey was that the "process" I was creating would soon help to create a template for what we now refer to as cyber counterintelligence, and that the U.S. government would eventually incorporate many of my own methods into its own attempts to track terrorism worldwide.

THERE IS NO QUESTION that my intelligence and creative ability allowed me to become an expert in this field. I was able to build a new, important kind of fort that fit very well my compartmentalized existence. As I have stated repeatedly, I didn't want any of this to interfere with my personal life. So I'm sure you're wondering why I am sharing my story and experience publicly. After all, the individuals that I was targeting in my quest were potential terrorists, or at least terrorist sympathizers. Simply put, once I became involved in the high-profile case involving Spec. Ryan G. Anderson, who provided the al-Qaeda terrorist network with sensitive and classified DoD information, I never again had the option to remain an anonymous counter-intelligence asset. It was never *my* decision or *my* intention to make my work public. And I have tried very hard in this book to protect the privacy of my family.

I eventually concluded that it was in my interests to make the best of a bad and unfortunate situation to the extent that I could. I had to conclude that being publicly known offered me a platform to continue making a difference in this world as well as an opportunity to promote the still developing field of cyber counterintelligence as a major resource for combating terrorism.

Do I really regret having gained name and professional recognition here at home and abroad? At first I did, maybe . . . but now, not really! My life today is what it is, and it is what it was always meant to be. I have come to peace with that now. When I look at my family, I am proud to say my children have fared well under the spotlight and with my occasional absences due to work. My two oldest kids are now adults and in college, starting the process of creating their own independent lives. My first child, my son, made me a grandmother on November 30, 2010. My youngest daughter was only seven on 9/11 and is now in the middle of her high school years.

Though I have devoted a significant amount of my time and life to combating the threat of terrorism since 9/11, I never sacrificed my relationship with my kids. I spent as much quality time as possible at home. I went to their choir and band concerts; I picked them up from practice. If they needed help with homework, I was always there. I did normal things too as a mom. I wasn't playing cyber spy all of the time. In some ways, that I have never learned to sleep well and have been able to survive on precious little amounts of sleep has allowed me to have time available to pursue my interests and important work where I might not otherwise have time available. It is amazing how three or four hours of time to oneself when most of the world is sleeping, or blessed with normal sleep habits, can make such a difference in one's life.

In closing this final chapter of this book, my message is quite simply this: Everyone has within them an ability to contribute to something larger than themselves—to effect change for the greater good. Please look within yourself and ask what it is you can do—what do you have to sacrifice? Opportunities abound to make the world a better place. Look at Greg Mortensen, a fellow Montanan, and the man who started new schools for young girls in Afghanistan. His journey to make Afghanistan a better place in this world began before 9/11 and continues to this day. Look at those who make financial contributions to the Young Warriors and the Wounded Warriors Project. And of course, if my life, sacrifice, and example so move you, you could consider joining the ever-growing field of cyber counterintelligence.

In writing this book, I wanted to take the opportunity to explain who I am and why I have done the things I did and where life has ultimately led me. I hope that, if people take anything away from my life experience and story, they will see things in a different light apart from the images and perceptions created by the news and media. It is also important to me that people who walk away from reading this book and learning about who the real Shannen Rossmiller is can believe that sometimes it's the little people in this world, and not necessarily the government or other important people in society, that can effect a change for the good of all. If people who read this book are able to find and recognize something in themselves that they can offer to make a difference in this world, then I will feel that it was worth stepping up and sacrificing aspects of my life to show that anyone can effect change if they truly look inside themselves and see that the impossible can be accomplished.

One of the reasons I decided to write this book was for closure and healing. There has always been so much speculation about me that I have wanted people to really know me and why I have done the things I have. I truly want to feel like all I have been through and sacrificed, and how my life was so drastically changed, will be respected and appreciated.

Stay safe and stay vigilant.

EPILOGUE

On Sunday, May 1, 2011, while this book was being edited for publication, President Obama announced that a team of U.S. Navy Seals conducted a covert mission in Abbottabad, Pakistan, killing Osama bin Laden. On hearing this news late that Sunday evening I felt numb and shocked—it seemed too surreal to be true. After almost ten years since that fateful day in September when bin Laden's al-Qaeda terrorist network flew planes into the World Trade Center Towers and the Pentagon, and in Shanksville, Pennsylvania, killing nearly 3,000 people, it just didn't seem possible that he was gone from this Earth forever.

In the following days I experienced a flood of conflicting emotions. Bin Laden and al-Qaeda are the very reasons I started down the path of pursuing terrorists, and though I was happy he was dead—especially at the hands of U.S. soldiers—I honestly felt some measure of disappointment that my long-standing target was no more. Back in 2003—when I began pursuing "Samir," the Arab journalist with close ties to bin Laden and al-Qaeda who became the premier target of Operation Whirlpool—I believed that one day I would find bin Laden through him.

In the aftermath of bin Laden's death, I decided to find out whether there was any news or information out there from Samir on this issue. I wasn't surprised to learn that on May 6, 2011, in an interview with the Italian website Bolognanotzie.com, Samir claimed that he had spoken with bin Laden's personal physician, who said that bin Laden had died a few days before the U.S. raid on bin Laden's compound, and that he had spoken to bin Laden many times over the years. Samir's claims, whether intended as propaganda or not, only bolstered my belief that my suspicions about his relationship to Public Enemy Number One had been on target, and that by pursuing Samir and his connections I may have eventually located bin Laden. At the time of writing this epilogue, ten days have passed since bin Laden was killed, and my feelings are slowly settling. The mass murderer who forever changed my beloved country finally paid the price for attacking the United States, and rightfully met his ultimate fate at U.S. hands. Yet his death has not brought me the closure I was expecting. After all, he was only one man, and he leaves behind one of the most prolific and effective terrorist organizations the world has ever known. I don't believe that I can have true closure until all of al-Qaeda is defeated, and that is where I will continue to focus my efforts. Until we have rooted out this lethal network in all its vast and complicated tentacles, my work to defeat them and the threat of terrorism will not be done, and the world should not let down its guard.

INDEX